COERCIVE CARE

A coherent and original approach to the important issue of coercion in care, and a significant contribution to the international bioethics debate.

Peter Singer, Monash University

Coercive Care: the ethics of choice in health and medicine asks probing and challenging questions regarding the use of coercion in health care and the social services. When is coercion legitimate and when is it illegitimate? Should HIV-positive people, with a 'dangerous' lifestyle, be put in custody? Is it morally acceptable to put a pregnant addict in custody in order to secure the health of her unborn child? If a person cannot stop abusing drugs, should she be treated, against her will, for her addiction?

The present volume argues for respect of the autonomy of the individual and refutes the system of paternalism whereby citizens are coerced into care in order to safeguard the interests of other people. The book combines philosophical analysis with comparative studies of social policy and law in a large number of industrialized countries and proposes an ideal of judicial security on a global scale.

Torbjörn Tännsjö deftly explores the multiple dimensions of the issue of coercion and breaks new ground in the debate of bioethics through his plea for the liberalization and harmonization of European, North American, Australian and Japanese laws regulating the use of coercion in care.

Torbjörn Tännsjö is Professor of Practical Philosophy at Gothenburg University, Sweden. He has published extensively in the fields of moral philosophy, political philosophy and bioethics.

COERCIVE CARE

The ethics of choice in health and medicine

Torbjörn Tännsjö

London and New York

174.2

T16c

First published 1999
by Routledge
11 New Fetter Lane, London EC4P 4EE

Simultaneously published in the USA and Canada
by Routledge
29 West 35th Street, New York, NY 10001

Routledge is an imprint of the Taylor & Francis Group

© 1999 Torbjörn Tännsjö

Typeset in Times by
BC Typesetting, Bristol
Printed and bound in Great Britain by
Biddles Ltd, Guildford and King's Lynn

British Library Cataloguing in Publication Data
A catalogue record for this book is available from the British Library

Library of Congress Cataloging in Publication Data
Tännsjö, Torbjörn, 1946–
Coercive care: the ethics of choice in health and medicine/
Torbjörn Tännsjö.
p.   cm.
Includes bibliographical references and index.
1. Involuntary treatment–Moral and ethical aspects.   I. Title.
IN PROCESS
174′.2–dc21   98-47880
                                               CIP

JK

ISBN 0–415–20849–1

CONTENTS

Preface   vi
Acknowledgements   ix

1   Introduction   1

2   Somatic health care   22

3   Preventive health care   55

4   Infectious diseases   80

5   Mental illness   89

6   Forensic psychiatry   105

7   Foetal/maternal conflicts   117

8   Coercion in the social services   129

9   Conclusion   138

Appendix: Convention on Human Rights and Biomedicine   141
Glossary   155
References   158
Index   162

PREFACE

In this book I discuss the legitimate role of coercive care in medicine and in the social services. I state and defend a principle of respect for the autonomy of the individual in decisions about medical care and social services.

The philosophical background of my discussion is very general. I take as my point of departure a general, utilitarian normative outlook. The choice of outlook is defended in Chapter 1. The factual background of the discussion, however, is international, if mainly Western. It is fair to say that the book is written from a Western perspective. As a matter of fact, I take as my point of departure rules valid in the US and Europe, and I give examples mainly from the US and the European countries. However, some Canadian, Australian and Japanese material is also presented and, for reasons to be stated later on, the book should be of special relevance to readers in Canada, Japan and Australia, as well as to US and European readers.

Of importance to my argument has been, of course, what has been stated in all sorts of *conventions* such as the European Convention. A main focus of my interest has been a new document, however, called the Convention on Human Rights and Biomedicine. This document, which throughout the book I will simply refer to as 'the Convention' has been reprinted at the end of the book. The Convention was adopted by the Committee of Ministers in the Council of Europe on 19 November 1996. Since the US, Australia, Canada and Japan also contributed to the Convention, legislative bodies in these countries will have to take a stand on it, which means that it will come to have world-wide importance.

In many respects the Convention is an admirable document. To be sure, it is the most advanced document in this field. There are some serious drawbacks even with this document, however.

First of all, being a kind of common denominator, on some controversial points it tends to avoid the problems rather than facing them head on. In this book I want to confront these controversial issues in particular.

Second, since the Convention has not yet been accepted, approved or ratified (these are the three possibilities given) by the member states, and since it is possible for the member states to make a reservation in respect of any particular provision of the Convention to the extent that any law then in force in its territory is not in conformity with that provision, it is uncertain what legal impact the Convention will come to have.

Finally, Article 26 of the Convention allows for restrictions of the exercise of the rights defined in the Convention. And it should be noted the Convention does not stipulate any sanctions against states that do not abide by it.

Yet, for all that, the impact that the Convention will have on biomedical discussions, and on public opinion, in the member states of the European Council (and in other countries which have contributed to it, such as Australia, Canada, Japan and the United States), will probably be considerable. My conjecture is that it will provide the starting point of a truly public and international discussion of bioethical questions. And my hope is that my book will make a real contribution to this discussion.

My book could be read as a plea for liberalisation and harmonisation of the European, North American, Australian, Canadian and Japanese laws regulating the use of coercion in care. I do not suggest any exact system of legal paragraphs, but I do provide a general framework for the development of such a system. And I indicate, in the examples given, where I think that the legal frameworks valid in the European countries and in the US (and, to some extent, in Canada, Australia and Japan) are in need of revision. However, it has been difficult to gather information about international law in this field and I am afraid that some of the things I say about laws in different countries may be inaccurate. The sources in this field seem to be notoriously unreliable, and the reality they describe is, of course, constantly changing. However, this should not be any real obstacle to my project, since my aim is normative, not descriptive. I make reference to existing law only in order to exemplify possible positions. So when mistaken descriptions are spotted, the reader is advised to inform the author about them, but not to get distracted from the main thrust of the argument of the book, which is normative.

In particular, I indicate how a harmonised legislation *should* be developed, respecting an ideal of anti-paternalism, honouring at the same time the ideal of judicial security. Both these ideals are explained in detail in Chapter 1 of the book.

The questions I raise and discuss are of a general nature, so I think it appropriate that countries like the European ones, the US, Canada, Japan and Australia, all industrially developed and with a high level of education, should be able to reach common solutions to them. Some such thought must also have been the driving force behind the efforts invested in the development of the Convention.

My project may seem overly ambitious, and so it is, in a rather obvious way. To my knowledge no book with a similar scope and aim exists. Of course, I do not have expertise on the factual aspects of all the fields I cover. As a matter of fact, being a professional philosopher, I have factual expertise on *none* of them. However, I have had the opportunity to discuss my ideas thoroughly with experts in all the fields where coercive care takes place. And by experts I mean not only care-givers, such as doctors, nurses, and social workers, or social scientists, lawyers and so forth, but patients and clients as well. Yet, for all that, I fully realise that what I give here is not the last word about any of the problems discussed.

I feel certain, however, that the questions I raise are of the utmost importance. They are of the utmost importance to people submitted to coercive care, of course, and to care-givers, who submit people to coercive care, but not only to them. They provide also a crucial test for the degree of civilisation of society as such, so they should be of concern to all of us.

A society that does not deal in a proper fashion with coercive care is either totalitarian, or, which is no better, callously complacent in relation to human suffering.

As citizens in democratic countries, we *all* have an obligation to see to it that neither one of these very serious mistakes is being perpetrated by the institutions we authorise through the political machinery in our own countries, in the EU, the US, or Australia, Canada or Japan.

I give my answers to the questions I raise after careful consideration. I give my answers in the belief that they are sound and in the hope that, to the extent that they are not, the discussion to come will prove me wrong.

ACKNOWLEDGEMENTS

In 1995 I published a book in Swedish about the appropriate role of coercion in care and I confronted Swedish legislation in the field with a principle of respect for the autonomy of the individual in decisions about medical care and social services stated and defended in the book. The present book has evolved out of the Swedish book. The main thrust of the argument is similar. However, this is no mere translation of the book previously published in Swedish.

I have had the opportunity of discussing that book with many experts in all the fields I cover with my argument. I have been to hospitals where people suffering from senile dementia or mental impairment are being treated for somatic diseases, to homes where people are being treated against their will for their drug problems, to closed psychiatric wards, to clinics providing forensic psychiatric care, to places where HIV-positive people have been compulsorily admitted and isolated, and so forth. I have discussed the questions raised in my book with patients, clients, doctors, social workers, lawyers, politicians, decision-makers and social scientists. I have learnt a great deal from all of these encounters. It is simply impossible to name all who have contributed to my argument.

Their comments have made me correct my argument on many points and they have shown me where it could and should be made more clear. However, the comments have not meant that I have changed my main thesis in this book.

On the contrary, even when my original conclusions may have seemed controversial, at least to the layman, they have been met with much interest and sympathy by people working in, or reflecting on, coercive care. These people have not all unanimously agreed with my argument. However, on each and every one of my main points, *some* of them have done so, and some have even provided me with further evidence for my position. This has, of course, increased my own belief in it.

Those who have argued against my position have helped me, on the other hand, to improve on it. They have not been successful in making me change my main position, but they have been no less helpful; their criticisms have saved me from many mistakes.

All this means that I am now capable of stating my argument once more, now in an international setting, in a new language, in a more comprehensive form and with an even stronger conviction that I am on the right track.

Many people have helped me to gather information about international law. In particular I would like to thank the Swedish judge Tor Sverne for providing me with material about European law in the field, and for having read and commented upon the penultimate draft of the entire manuscript;[1] the psychiatrists Lars Kjellin and Helena Silfverhielm, who have both guided me in my search for material about the legal situation in the Western world with respect to psychiatric care; the forensic psychiatrist Sten Levander who has helped me with literature and insights about the possibility of predicting the actual dangerousness of those regarded as the 'dangerous insane'; the social scientist Anders Bergmark, who has provided me with data about coercive treatment of drug addicted people; and Angela J. Schneider, at the Faculty of Health Sciences, University of Western Ontario, who has helped me with information about coercive measures taken against drug abusing pregnant women in Canada.

I would also like to thank Hans Mathlein, Christian Munthe, Lars Sandman and Peter Singer, as well as an anonymous reviewer for Routledge, who have all commented on the penultimate draft of my manuscript. I have greatly benefited from their constructive criticisms.

A section on coercion in somatic care of people suffering from senile dementia or mental retardation in Chapter 1 is based on an article that has appeared in *Nursing Ethics* (Tännsjö 1999). And Chapter 6 is based on a previously published article, which has appeared in the journal *Bioethics* (Tännsjö 1997). I thank the editors for allowing me to use the material in the present context. No other part of the book has been previously published in any form.

I initiated the work in this field when I held a position as senior researcher at the Swedish Council for Research in the Humanities and Social Sciences. The Council has also supported the publication of the book. For all this I am thankful.

1 Many of my observations about the legal situation in Europe, and in some European countries in particular (Spain, the Netherlands and the UK), are taken from his 'Comments on the Legislation Concerning Impaired Capacity and Decision-Making in the Health Care Field in England and Wales, the Netherlands, Spain and Sweden' (1997).

1

INTRODUCTION

There are situations where the use of coercive care is appropriate. Society sometimes has to allow that medical or other kinds of treatment be *forced* upon patients who desperately need to be treated, but who refuse to undergo the needed treatment voluntarily. And, although this may be a shocking thing to say, society ought to sanction that sometimes patients and clients be in various different ways *manipulated* to receive the treatment they desperately need but refuse to accept voluntarily. Society ought to countenance the fact that sometimes patients should have their medicine smuggled into them, through their food, for example. This point will be argued in this book; however, in its most general form, it seems to me too obvious really to need any argument. Unless such measures are *sometimes* taken, society will fail to live up to simple humanitarian standards.

However, in handling coercive care, society may (only too easily) go wrong. There are two ways in which society may err. Society may err, on the one hand, in being only too willing to allow coercive care; society may allow coercive care where it should prohibit it. Society may err, on the other hand, in being too restrictive in allowing coercive care, prohibiting coercive care where it ought actually to take place. In the first case, society may come to slide into totalitarianism. In the second, it may become inhumane, tolerating unnecessary suffering and even death.

Obviously, one and the same society may, at one and the same time, make both kinds of mistake, and become both totalitarian and inhumane. So it is of crucial importance to learn where to draw the line. The objective of this book is to contribute to this discussion. I intend to investigate when society should, and when society should not, tolerate and encourage the use of coercive care.

The result of my study is a principled stance towards the problem. I defend an exact way of drawing the line, allowing for some instances of coercive care, repudiating others. In particular, I argue that, in order to be legitimate, coercive care must be compatible with what I will define as 'the principle of respect for the autonomy of the individual in decisions about medical care and social services'.

1

My interest is very general. I examine all possible kinds of care: medical care (both preventive and curative, both somatic and psychiatric), care in relation to punishment, care in relation to defence against infectious disease, foetal/maternal conflicts and care in relation to drug addiction as provided within the social services.

Point of departure

My point of departure is straightforwardly utilitarian. I want to investigate what system of coercive health care has the best effects, on the whole, for people living with it.

I will not try to show that utilitarianism is the best moral system. I have done so elsewhere (see Tännsjö 1998) but, more importantly, this is not crucial to my objective in the present context. Almost all people (all decent people?) seem to agree that there is *something* to utilitarianism. At least, they admit, we ought to take the action with the best consequences in *the most* situations. We ought to pay *some* attention to the value of the consequences of our actions. At least, they admit, we ought to maximise happiness or satisfaction if the cost to us (*qua* agents) is moderate and if there are no other strong considerations against doing so.

This means that, if, taking utilitarianism as my point of departure, I were to defend a system of coercive care allowing for *a great deal of* social interference with the individual, and for much licence in the handling by the medical authorities of individuals, then I would be open to the reply: 'Well, you have reached your conclusion only because you have taken for granted that the end justifies the means!'

However, if I end up with a restrictive system of coercive care, allowing for coercive care only under very special and narrowly circumscribed circumstances, then there is no room for any objection of this kind.

Now, this is what I will in fact do. From a very narrow point of departure (simple hedonistic utilitarianism) I end up with a very restrictive view of the use of coercive care.

This fact, that a restrictive view of coercive care can be defended on strictly utilitarian grounds, may seem remarkable and therefore interesting as such. And this fact provides us, if my argument is correct, with a very strong case for a restrictive system of coercive care, since my argument is based on so few basic assumptions, and, in particular, on no controversial ones at all.

Those who believe in basic human rights, for example, should have nothing to complain about in my conclusions; rather, they may add further arguments for them.

A practical problem with utilitarianism, which has often been pointed out, is that it provides us with only a criterion of rightness, not a method of decision-making. To be sure, it would not be wise to recommend that people always calculate and try to take the action with the best consequences. We never know which action this is.

It might be somewhat better advice to say that people should take the action that they believe maximises *expected* happiness, taking both probabilities and values into account. But even this will not do as a general recommendation. In particular, when we are dealing with a society and its relation to its citizens, we want to have legal *rules* determining what can and cannot be done by the authorities.

We do not want the judge or the doctor, the nurse or the social worker to perform, in each situation, the action he or she believes maximises expected happiness. Such a system would result in many arbitrary and strange decisions. We want nothing of the kind. We want to be able to *predict* their behaviour.

This is why we want to have their behaviour regulated through laws and in other, more informal, ways. But we do want to have it regulated by a system of laws and practices such that, when we adopt it and abide by it, to the degree that we actually do, it produces the best possible consequences. At least we want to have it regulated by such a system, if the system is consistent with (and protects) various possible, putative individual rights.

Can we say anything more general about what such a system of rules regulating the use of coercive care should look like? I think we can. Even if we take a narrow, utilitarian point of departure for our argument, we can give good reasons for the claim that the system of rules should satisfy two important requirements.

First, the system should live up to strong standards of *judicial security*. And, second, the system should respect an ideal of *anti-paternalism*. When these two desiderata are met, we have, I will say, a system that itself respects the principle of respect for the autonomy of the individual in decisions about medical care and social services.

I will now explain these claims in detail.

Judicial security

Judicial security is a matter both of procedure and of the content of laws. Among the requirements of procedure are that people be tried personally (habeas corpus) before being subjected to coercive care, that their case be tried without unnecessary delay, that they be guaranteed a competent defence, that they and their attorney be informed of all the details of their case.

Among the requirements of content, three stand out as the most important ones (I refer to them as the three 'C's' of the ideal of judicial security).

First of all, the laws regulating the use of coercive care must be cast in *clear* (and unambiguous) terms. This is the requirement of clarity.

Second, the laws regulating the use of coercive care must meet a requirement of *consistency* (the statutes must be consistent internally, they must
be consistent with each other and they must be consistent in *practice*).

The requirements that the statutes be consistent internally and together
with each other are formal (logical). The requirement that the statutes be
consistent in practice is material; there should exist *no* situation where,
according to one statute, a person should be submitted to coercive care
while, according to another statute, the same person should not be submitted to coercive care.

Third, the laws regulating the use of coercive care must meet a requirement of *consequentiality*. This means that, if, on certain grounds, one
person in one situation can (or cannot) be subjected to coercive care, then
the same should be true of any other person (irrespective of social status,
diagnosis and so forth). Equal cases should be treated on an equal basis.

The (utilitarian) rationale behind the requirements of judicial security,
both the requirements of procedure and the requirements of content, is the
fact that, unless they are met, we will *all* feel, *all* the time, somewhat
uneasy.

Qua citizens, we want to be able to *predict* whether we will be subjected
to coercive treatment or not. This means that the system of rules regulating
the use of coercive care must meet the requirements of clarity and consistency. Moreover, we care about fairness. If two cases are in relevant
respects similar, then we want society to treat them in a similar way; we do
not want to accept that one person be treated coercively where another
person, in a similar situation (but with, for example, another diagnosis), is
not coercively treated; this is the rationale behind the requirement of
consequentiality.

Furthermore, if a situation emerged where we might be submitted to
coercive care, we want no mistake to be made. The system of law should
be administered in a meticulous manner and it should be subject to public
review. This means that the requirements of procedure must be met.

Further arguments for the ideal of judicial security, referring for
example to the rights of individuals, could be given, but since a sound and
simple utilitarian rationale exists for the ideal, there is no need to go into
these (more controversial) arguments.

I will say no more about the ideal of judicial security. The claim that
society should do its best to see to it that the ideal of judicial security be
respected does not strike me as very controversial. Not that society always
lives up to the ideal – it often flouts it, as a matter of fact. But I think few
are prepared to *defend* this, if it is pointed out and acknowledged. I turn
therefore to what I think *is* controversial, namely the desideratum that the
system of rules regulating coercive care should satisfy an ideal of anti-
paternalism.

4

The ideal of anti-paternalism

In my principled rejection of paternalism I follow J.S. Mill whose view is stated most clearly in *On Liberty*. However, my interest is systematic, not historic.

There may exist some slight differences between his anti-paternalist stance and mine, but I will not go into these problems here. Some of the differences of opinion will be discussed in context, in chapters to come. Others will not be commented upon at all. My account stands on its own feet and should be assessed for what it is. I will refer to it as the ideal of anti-paternalism.

According to the ideal of anti-paternalism, when applied to the health care field, people who have reached the age of maturity and who are capable of making an autonomous decision whether to accept a proposed treatment or not, and who reject the treatment in question, should not, in *their own best interest*, be forced to undergo the treatment. These people should be guaranteed an absolute right to a veto against whatever kind of treatment considered necessary for them, be it curative or preventive, be it directed against somatic illness, mental illness or drug abuse.

I return below to J.S. Mill's arguments for this principle. Before that I will state the principle of respect for the autonomy of the individual in decisions about medical care and social services, based on the ideal of respect for judicial security as well as on the ideal of anti-paternalism.

Respect for autonomy

This is my (preliminary) statement of the principle of respect for the autonomy of the individual in decisions about medical care and social services, based both on the ideal of judicial security and on the ideal of anti-paternalism:

> Society should never tolerate that patients and clients, who are adult and capable of making their own autonomous decisions, be coerced into accepting any kind of care.

Part of the rationale behind the principle is, in an obvious manner, anti-paternalistic. However, the principle of respect for the autonomy of the individual in decisions about medical care and social services goes beyond an anti-paternalistic insistence that people should not, merely in their own best interest, be submitted to coercive care; the principle states also that people should not *in the interest of others* be subjected to coercive care.

This additional aspect of the principle has nothing to do with anti-paternalism. Even Mill accepts that people be coerced in some situations, in order to stop them from harming others. I agree about this, of course. However, and this is *my* claim, when a person is coerced in the interest of another person, the means used should never be *care*; people who are competent to make their own decisions should *never* be subjected to coercive care of *any* kind.

If they have proved to be dangerous to others, even because of some mental disorder, say, this may be a reason to put them in gaol, but not for *treating* them, against their will, for their mental disorder.

The rationale behind this (further) part of the principle has to do with the ideal of judicial security and with a general idea that it is of the utmost importance that society draws a very sharp demarcation line between, on the one hand, care, and, on the other hand, punishment.

Of course, people may well be coerced in various ways by society in order to safeguard the interests of *other* people. In a civilised society, no one should be allowed to *harm* other people. However, when (preventive) force is used against a person in the interest of others (to prevent harm to others), then the aim of the force should never be treatment.

If the aim is treatment, for the sake of others, then there is a definite risk that the treatment will not actually be in the best interest of the person coerced. If the intentions with the care are mixed (to cure the person, to be sure, but also, and more importantly, to make the person harmless), then this may mean that we do things to this individual that are *harmful* to him. And even if this is not actually the case, the individual in question may well come to *suspect* that it is. Such suspicions, which are very difficult to silence, may prove very damaging to the health care system as such.

To take an obvious example. If a person has been convicted for having committed paedophilic crimes, it may be tempting for society to offer this person medical castration. This may be what this person wants, and then it would be proper to provide it. However, if the person rejects this treatment, society should not force it upon him. Instead he should be incapacitated through incarceration, and he should be provided with the *option* of choosing medical castration, whenever he sees fit to do so.

The sanction against dangerous persons should be incarceration, not care. Care should be provided on a voluntary basis, for those who need it and demand it. It should not be part of the punishment.

And in a society honouring the ideal of judicial security, the punishment should always be meted out for a criminal offence *actually committed* by a person, not on predictive grounds (not on the grounds that, in the future, the person may *come* to commit the crime in question).

Predictions of the dangerousness of a person are notoriously difficult to make. Predictions of how such predictions will turn out are even more difficult to make. That is why such predictions should not be the basis of compulsory commitment. If they are, we as a public cannot know for sure whether we will be detained or not, if we choose a certain lifestyle.

We as a public *must* be able to know this: we must be able to know how to behave in order not to be compulsorily detained. This is part of the ideal of judicial security.

The status of the principle

There are many points that must be clarified in the rough statement given here of the principle of respect for the autonomy of the individual in decisions about medical care and social services. The rationale behind it (provided by the ideals of judicial security and anti-paternalism) is also in need of some explanation.

Before I go into explaining all these points, it must be noted that my intention is not to state a fundamental moral principle. My defence of the principle is indirect. The principle of respect for the autonomy of the individual in decisions about medical care and social services is not the premiss of my argument, but the conclusion of it. I conjecture that, if the ideal be respected, then, on the whole, we will have a better system of coercive care than we would have if the ideal was not respected.

This is a bold empirical conjecture. It cannot be grasped a priori. As a matter of fact, this entire book is devoted to the *piecemeal* task of defending it.

In my book I will consider all possible kinds of coercive care and I will argue, for each kind, that, if the principle of respect for the autonomy of the individual in decisions about medical care and social services be met, the consequences will be (on the whole) better than if it is not met.

This does not mean that I intend to show that in *each* case, the consequences of living up to the principle of respect for the autonomy of the individual in decisions about medical care and social services are better than they would be if an aberration from it was made. *No* system of rules can safeguard that, in each case, the right decision will be made. *All* systems of rules are more or less defective in this respect.

My conjecture is only that, if the principle of respect for the autonomy of the individual in decisions about medical care and social services be met, then the consequences *on the whole* will be better than if it is not met. My conjecture is that, if the principle of respect for the autonomy of the individual in decisions about medical care and social services be respected, then the cases where people, who should really have been coercively treated, but were not so treated, and the cases where people who should really not have been coercively treated, but were so treated, *are kept at a minimum.*

Why not children?

My principle of respect for the autonomy of the individual in decisions about medical care and social services does not cover children. Why not?

The answer is easy and obvious. Children may sometimes be able to make autonomous decisions concerning their own medical needs, but, in general, they are not capable of taking wise decisions.

We should involve children in medical decisions concerning their own medical needs, and we can perhaps trust their opinion to a much larger extent than we actually do. Furthermore, children should be *taught* to make wise decisions. This takes some training. However, it would not be wise to grant children an absolute right to have their own way in their own medical matters.

Where are we to draw the line?

This is not a matter of principle. We have to draw it in such a manner that we can be sure that we do not put their life and health unnecessarily in jeopardy. We need a line that is salient. However, the exact line must be arbitrary, in exactly the same manner that a speed limit must be arbitrary. This is an arbitrariness that we are used to living with.

It is only natural to exclude children from the principle of respect for the autonomy of the individual in decisions about medical care and social services, when the ideal is arrived at as the conclusion of a moral argument, not as a premiss of it. For principled libertarians, who believe that liberty is of value as such, things are more complicated, however.

Principled libertarians honour liberty irrespective of the consequences. So they cannot argue that children should not decide about their medical or social needs simply because children may make unwise decisions. They have to argue that children cannot make autonomous decisions at all, that children are, as it were, not genuine persons.

It is no easy task to show this, but, since I do not rely on libertarian principles in my defence of the principle of respect for the autonomy of the individual in decisions about medical care and social services, I need not go any further into these problems.

The principle explained in detail

There are many points of detail in my statement of the principle of respect for the autonomy of the individual in decisions about medical care and social services that are in need of clarification. In particular, it is important to draw a line between, on the one hand, illegitimate *coercion* and, on the other hand, various kinds of acceptable *persuasion*. And it is of the utmost importance to state more in detail what it means for a person to be *capable of reaching his or her own autonomous decision*.

I now proceed to a clarification of the difference between coercion and persuasion. My next objective will be to explain what it means for a person to be able to reach his or her own decision about whether or not to accept a proposed treatment.

After having clarified my principle of respect for the autonomy of the individual in decisions about medical care and social services I turn to a recapitulation of J.S. Mill's important defence of his anti-paternalistic stance, also relevant to my purposes.

Coercion vs. persuasion

How are we to draw the line between coercion and persuasion? We should draw it in terms of the intention behind the measure taken, I suggest.

I use the word 'intention' in a slightly technical sense. The intention *may* be something mental, it may be part of the mental life of the person exercising coercion or doing the persuading. This is a standard use of the term. But an intention may also be something *institutional*. And this makes my use of the term technical.

The intention may be institutional in particular where some *authority* performs a certain action, affecting an individual. Then there may exist an explicit or implicit intention with the action, which can be read off from statutes of law, or from expressed intentions behind these laws, or from the application of them, and so forth, rather than from the inner mental life of the person acting on behalf of these laws.

In terms of this notion of an intention we can now make the following demarcation. An agent may in various ways affect the decisions of another person. Some of these ways are not at all coercive. A doctor may, for example, by his or her reasoning, by his or her example, or simply by his or her authority, *make* a patient accept a certain proposed treatment. This may be persuasion rather than rational argument, but it need not be coercion. It *is* a case of coercive care, however, when, intentionally, through the use of force, or threats, or manipulation, or positive incentives (or gratifications), the person is made to accept (or simply to undergo) a certain treatment *he or she does not want to undergo* (in the absence of the force, the threat, or the incentives, or gratifications).

It is not coercion to inform a patient that, unless he or she accepts a proposed treatment, he or she will probably die. It is coercion, however, to threaten a patient that, if he or she does not take part in a certain medical trial, he or she will receive *worse* treatment.

It is not coercion to inform a person that, if he undergoes medical castration, he will be out of prison earlier than if he does not. It is coercion, however, if something extra is added to his punishment *in order* to make him more willing to undergo castration.

Manipulation is included in my slightly technical sense of 'coercion', and it is of special interest here. How do we draw the line between legitimate influence and manipulation?

The crucial difference lies in the perception, on the part of the doctor, or nurse, or social worker, of the patient's and client's *own* idea of relevance of different pieces of information.

It is appropriate, and not manipulation, when a doctor, or nurse, or social worker, stresses pieces of information that he or she believes to be of great relevance to the decision to be taken by the patient or client ('Unless you undergo the cure, there is a not negligible risk that you will die!', for example).

However, if the doctor, or nurse, or social worker, suspects that a certain piece of information, not positively relevant, in the eyes of the doctor, or nurse, or social worker, is positively relevant *in the eyes of the patient or client*, for a certain decision, and if the doctor, or nurse, or social worker, in order to avoid that the patient or client takes the decision in question, withholds this piece of information, then this is manipulation. Subterfuge is included in 'manipulation' as I use the term, and manipulation is included in my technical sense of 'coercion'.

It is also manipulation to allow a patient to remain ignorant of something the doctor, or nurse, or social worker, knows would make the patient or client reach a decision which is, in the eyes of the doctor, or nurse, or social worker, the wrong one.

The doctor, or nurse, or social worker, has a twofold pedagogical task: all the facts relevant, in the eyes of the doctor, or nurse, or social worker, to the patient's or client's case, should be brought forward and explained to the patient or client. The doctor, or nurse, or social worker, must make sure that the patient or client 'gets' the message.

But this is not enough. All the facts relevant, *in the eyes of the patient or client*, to the extent that it is possible for the doctor, or nurse, or social worker to acknowledge them, should be brought forward as well.

Otherwise we will have a case of manipulation (and so a case of 'coercion', in my sense of the term) of the patient or client by the doctor, or nurse, or social worker.

The capacity to decide autonomously

What does it mean (in the present context) for a person to be able to decide autonomously for himself or herself whether to accept a proposed treatment or not? Clearly, what we are in need of here is an *explication* of the notion, not a report of ordinary usage.

I intend to stipulate a meaning. And my objective is to stipulate a meaning which makes the principle of respect for the autonomy of the individual in decisions about medical care and social services as plausible and fruitful as possible. This means that, on the one hand, I must avoid a stipulation that makes the principle obviously *unacceptable*, and, on the other hand, I must avoid a stipulation that makes the ideal *trivial*.

A way of making the principle of respect for the autonomy of the individual in decisions about medical care and social services obviously *unacceptable* would be to take a person to possess a capacity for reaching his or her autonomous decision as soon as the person can *say* 'yes' or 'no', when asked whether he or she wants to undergo a certain treatment. Even a severely mentally disturbed person, in the grips of 'voices', and in desperate need of medical care, can say 'yes' or 'no' to a proposed treatment (such as life-saving surgery). But it is not obvious that his or her 'no' should be taken for an answer.

A way of making the principle of respect for the autonomy of the individual in decisions about medical care and social services *trivial* would be to take a person to lack capacity for reaching his or her own decision as soon as the decision itself is found wanting (by the doctor, or nurse, or the social worker and so forth). This would mean that the principle of respect for the autonomy of the individual in decisions about medical care and social services would not grant the patients and clients any protection at all against doctors, nurses, social workers and so forth. So even if no one could object to it, there would be no need for it.

We therefore need to try to find a sense of 'capable of reaching one's own autonomous decisions' which is compatible with the patient and client, in some circumstances, at least, reaching a decision which is *not* applauded by the doctor, or nurse, or social worker – a decision which, for all that, deserves to be taken seriously.

Let me now say in more detail when I consider a person capable of reaching his or her own autonomous decision. This is a matter of his or her *capacity* to make decisions, not a matter of the content of these decisions themselves.

First of all, in order to be capable or reaching his or her own autonomous decision (in the sense relevant in the present context, of course – I will omit explicitly stating this from now on) the person must be capable of conceiving of himself or herself as an *agent*. For example, he or she must not believe that he or she is just an instrument in the hands of some strange 'powers'. He or she must realise that, in the situation, various different options are open, and it depends on the person him- or her*self* what option be chosen. She must recognise, for example, that she can accept, or that she can reject, a certain proposed treatment.

Second, this individual must recognise that, depending on his or her choice, various different *outcomes* are possible. To some extent these outcomes depend on the individual himself or herself (on his or her decision), of course, but he or she is not omnipotent. He or she must recognise this. He or she must recognise that the outcomes of his or her actions depend also on what *other* people do, and on the existing *state of nature*. If she accepts the proposed treatment she may be cured, but there is also a possibility that she will be hurt by the treatment, the treatment may furthermore be harmless but useless, and so forth. In order to be able to reach an autonomous decision of her own, she must be capable of conceiving of these kinds of possibilities.

Third, not only must the individual recognise that different outcomes of her choice are possible, he or she must also have some view about how *likely*, depending on what he or she does, these possible outcomes are. He or she need not make numerical estimates of probabilities (summing to 1), of course (we rarely do) but he or she must have at least *some* hints about some outcomes being more or less likely than others, some being more likely if a certain proposed treatment is accepted than if it is not accepted, and so forth.

Fourth, not only must the individual recognise that different outcomes are more or less likely, depending on how he or she acts, he or she must also be capable of forming an idea about how *desirable* the various possible outcomes are.

Fifth, the individual must be capable of applying some sort of decision rule, weighing together (somehow) values and probabilities, into a *decision*.

Sixth, this decision must be *effective*. This means that the agent must be capable of carrying this decision out in action. There could be some room for akrasia (weakness of will), of course, but not a total akrasia. A person who decides not to steal, who goes into the shop, comes out of it, and 'finds' that he or she has stolen something, is not capable of making his or her autonomous decisions (in this respect). A person who decides not to take drugs but who still takes them, when he or she has an opportunity to do so, is likewise not capable of making his or her autonomous decisions (in this respect). The autonomous agent does not act compulsively.

Seventh, the person needs to be able to *modify* his or her beliefs and values in the light of arguments and new experiences. His or her beliefs and values must not as such have a compulsive nature. A person who rejects a suggested treatment because he or she believes that the medicine has been contaminated should not for this reason alone be considered incapable of reaching his or her own decision, no matter how unlikely it is that the medicine has actually been contaminated. However, if the patient rejects the treatment because she believes that the CIA has contaminated the medicine, *and if this belief is immune to reflection*, i.e. if it has a *compulsive* nature, if it is what the 'voices' inform her, then her 'no' to the medicine need not be taken at face value. In the circumstances, she is not capable of reaching a decision about whether to undergo the proposed treatment or not. Perhaps a decision should be taken *for* her (in her own best interest).

What has here been said about beliefs applies to values as well. If a person decides to take considerable risks, in order to realise some strange value, such as being the first to climb a certain mountain, society should honour his or her decision. However, if a person has a *compulsive* wish always to be 'clean', and decides to stay in the shower all day long, this decision need not be honoured by society. In some circumstances, such a person may be taken out of the shower, in his or her own best interest.

Now, all this may begin to look threatening. These seven requirements may seem very severe. The reader may come to wonder whether he or she is capable of reaching his or her own autonomous decisions. Have I not gone too far? Have I not made the principle of respect for the autonomy of the individual in decisions about medical care and social services trivial by making it almost *impossible* for a patient or client to reach a decision not to accept a suggested treatment that is worthy of his or her doctor's or social worker's respect?

I think not. And it is crucial to my argument that I haven't. So let me point out also that there are several aspects of the notion of a capacity for autonomous decision-making, playing the role of 'extenuating circumstances', rendering it easy for most (ordinary) persons in most (ordinary) situations to possess the capacity in question.

Let me briefly state some of these extenuating circumstances.

Extenuating circumstances

It is true of most (perhaps all) persons that in many situations we do not reach our decisions in the manner indicated above. We do not conceive of ourselves as agents (but put our hope in fate), we do not contemplate possible outcomes (but take only one outcome into consideration), we make no assessments of probabilities, we do not articulate our values, we do not consciously apply any decision method: we just make a decision. Or, we just act (out of habit, for example, or, because someone tells us what to do). This does not mean that society is allowed to force treatment upon us, if we refuse to accept it. The crucial thing is not that we *exercise* our capacity to make a decision, the crucial thing is that we *possess* it.

It may well be that we have a capacity to make a decision but simply refuse to use it. If we do, our doctor, or nurse, or social worker, should urge us to consider the consequences. However, even if we don't consider the consequences, we should be allowed to have our say. Provided, of course, that we could (if we wanted) make an autonomous decision.

This claim of mine is crucial to my argument, but not uncontroversial, so a brief comment will be made about it here (in the manner of foreshadowing arguments in chapters to come).

Why accept poor reasoning?

It might be thought that, if a person, capable of reaching an autonomous decision, reaches a decision based on poor argument and on values that are not 'genuinely' her own, simply because he or she does not bother to reflect on the matter more thoroughly, her 'no', at least her 'no' to life-saving treatment, should be overruled, in her own best interest.

This very popular line has famously been taken by, for example, Bruce L. Miller (1983) in order to grant that medical reasons take priority when a patient behaves imprudently because of poor reasoning or lack of contact with her own deepest interests. According to Miller, a 'no' from a competent but irrational or less than authentic patient should sometimes be overruled by a care-giver. It should be overruled in the best interests of the patient. However, for reasons to be stated more explicitly later on, I will have none of this. This is a rough outline of my argument.

First of all, if we strengthen the requirements to be met by a person in order to deserve respect for his or her decisions, in the manner indicated by Miller, then we make the principle of respect for autonomy *useless*. Even if it were respected, it would not grant that people in general could approach the health care system with any confidence that they would have their way. If, according to their doctor, nurse or social worker, their decisions were considered imprudent, there would be a definite risk that their refusal to accept treatment would not be respected. The doctor, nurse or social worker may claim that there is something wrong with their reasoning, or that their decision is not authentic, not 'really' their own.

It is crucial to my argument from trust that most grown up people, in ordinary circumstances, when mentally healthy, not suffering from senile dementia or mental impairment, should feel certain that their decisions about their own medical or social needs will be respected by a doctor (or nurse, or social worker), no matter what the doctor (or nurse, or social worker) may think about it.

Second, strong arguments from judicial security, and from the requirement of consequentiality in particular, speak in favour of not strengthening the requirements to be met by a person in order for the person to have his or her decisions respected within the health care and social systems. After all, we do not require sound arguments and a contact with 'true' values and interests in decisions *other* than medical and social ones, even if the consequences of them are very severe indeed. So why require it in the social and medical contexts? It would be unfair to treat medical and social decisions differently.

We allow people to climb mountains, swim rivers and so forth, and put their life in jeopardy. Some give away all their money. We do not require that their decisions to do so be based on sound argument or true values. Thus, in the interests of fairness, we should require no more of arguments leading up to medical decisions by mentally healthy, grown up, people.

Further extenuating circumstances

It is true of most (perhaps all) persons, furthermore, that there are some situations where they cannot decide autonomously for themselves what to do. This may make it legitimate for society, in the circumstances, to coerce them into some kind of treatment. However, this does not mean that society should allow that they be coercively treated in *other* situations.

To take one important example. Suppose a person cannot help drinking alcohol, when he has an opportunity to do so. When he can drink alcohol he 'finds' himself drinking. This means that he cannot reject an offered drink. This does not mean, however, that this person cannot make an autonomous decision as to whether he should accept a proposed cure for his alcoholism or not.

Both this consideration, and the one made previously, namely that it is the *capacity* to make autonomous decisions, not the actual *exercise* of it, that matters, help to explain why there may be situations where a patient's or client's 'no' to a treatment should be taken for an answer. Here are some further considerations to the same effect.

Unless a person can decide for him- or herself how desirable and how probable various possible outcomes of his or her actions in a situation are, he or she cannot make an autonomous decision (in the situation). However, the values are his or her *own*, and so are his or her beliefs about probability.

Provided the values and beliefs of the person are open to critical reflection (and revision in the light of arguments and new experiences), they are to be taken at face value by the doctor, or nurse, or social worker.

People make very different assessments about what is of value to them, and the amount of risk aversion varies in a bewildering way between people. This is not seen as a problem outside health care. Once again, people are allowed to climb mountains and to ride motorcycles. Thus they should be allowed to take their chances within the health care system, putting their life and health at stake, for whatever reasons they themselves see fit.

The doctor, or nurse, may find it outrageous when a patient chooses to die from gangrene in a leg, rather than agreeing to undergo an amputation. However, if this is the choice the patient makes, then this choice should be respected by the doctor, or nurse, or so I am prepared to argue. The patient should be allowed to die from his or her disease, and, if he or she does choose to do so, he or she should be compassionately and professionally cared for, *while* dying.

J.S. Mill's reasons against paternalism

Why ought we to respect the autonomy of the patients and clients within our systems of health and social care?

I have already indicated that this matter cannot be settled a priori. It is a matter of the relative efficacy of different possible systems of rules.

However, there are some general considerations indicating that at least a strong presumption exists for allowing adult people, who can make their own decisions about their need for health and social care, to have their own say, as far as *their own* interest goes. These arguments were stated clearly by J.S. Mill in his *On Liberty*. They are as follows.

First of all, the individual has a *special interest* in his or her own life, that is not shared by other people. Mill writes as follows:

> neither one person, nor any number of persons, is warranted in saying to another human creature of ripe years, that he shall not do with his life for his own benefit what he chooses to do with it. He is the person most interested in his own well-being: the interest which any other person, except in cases of strong personal attachment, can have in it, is trifling, compared with that which he himself has . . .
>
> (Mill 1973: 206)

This special interest is obvious in matters of health care and social services. The doctor, or nurse, or social worker, may to some extent sympathise with their patients and clients, but there is, should be and must be, a limit to sympathy. When work time is up the doctor, or nurse, or social worker goes home. Apart from suicide, however, one cannot 'walk away' from one's own life. Each person has to live their own life.

Second, not only does the individual have a special interest in his or her own life, he or she has special expertise as well, a privileged epistemological position. To quote Mill once more:

> with respect to his own feelings and circumstances, the most ordinary man or woman has means of knowledge immeasurably surpassing those that can be possessed by any one else.
>
> (1973: 206–207)

This privileged epistemological position may perhaps be questioned when it comes to medical decisions. Does not the doctor know better than the patient about the medical status of the patient? He or she undoubtedly does. However, this is a kind of knowledge that the doctor should be able to communicate to the patient, in all relevant respects. The expertise of the patient concerns, not the medical facts but, as Mill puts it, 'his own feelings and circumstances'. These may be of vital importance to the decision about treatment, and in contradistinction to medical facts, they may be hard to communicate. Moreover, the patient may be unwilling to communicate them. And while the doctor can (and should) be put under an obligation to communicate the medical facts to the patient, the patient

16

cannot plausibly be put under any corresponding obligation to communicate 'his own feelings and circumstances' to the doctor.

Finally, in his argument Mill takes for granted that there is a *price* to be paid when someone is coerced into a way of living. This is true in general and it is all the more true in the medical and social context. It is not nice to be subjected to coercion, nor is it nice in general (nor *should* it be nice) to coerce others.

To this we could add a closely related consideration. There is in most cases a *therapeutic* gain to be made from measures that are freely chosen by a patient or client. This is true in particular, when the 'cure' involves, as is the case for example in treatment against drug addiction, some kind of transformation or change of the character or personality of the patient or client.

These three considerations do not 'settle the case' in favour of my principle of respect for the autonomy of the individual in decisions about medical care and social services. As has been stressed several times before, there is no a priori way to settle it. However, together with what has been said above about the importance of making a sharp separation between punishment and care, these considerations do create a strong *presumption* that, in general, the autonomous decision of an adult person about what kind of care to accept should be honoured by society.

Could the patient demand the kind of treatment he or she sees fit?

It should be noted that the principle of respect for the autonomy of the individual in decisions about medical care and social services has a negative form. It grants the right of the patient or client to reject a suggested kind of treatment. It does not imply that the patient or client has a right to whatever treatment he or she sees fit to demand.

I do not believe in any such (positive) right. Society must take responsibility for what kinds of cures it offers to prospective patients and clients. The cures that can be offered to patients and clients must stand up to severe tests for efficacy and security. They must be in conformity with both science and medical experience.

Furthermore, in a publicly financed health and social care system, political authorities are responsible for a sound allocation of medical resources and social services. This too means that there can be no 'right to choose' on the part of the patients or clients, at least not *within* the publicly financed system.

It is a difficult and delicate matter to draw lines here. What kinds of 'alternative' cures, considered harmless by society, should be tolerated, and what kinds of cures, considered positively dangerous, should be prohibited? To what extent should a publicly financed health care system finance 'alternative' medical measures?

Another delicate problem is the clinical testing of new drugs. A new drug may provide hope for a person with a serious and hitherto incurable disease. However, the drug may be dangerous. To what extent could the decision be left to the patient of whether the possible gain makes the risk worth taking? To what extent must it be taken by society and by medical authorities? These are problems that lie outside the scope of the present book, however.[1]

My sole aim is to defend a more *restricted* and *negative* principle of respect for the autonomy of the individual in decisions about those health care measures and those social services that are actually provided for, or simply allowed to exist, by society.

The state of the art

As we have seen, crucial to my argument is the notion of personal autonomy, and the idea that personal autonomy be respected. As we have also seen, J.S. Mill had some important things to say, in *On Liberty*, about this idea. Without going into historical detail, and without following him in all respects, I have, as it were, taken his ideas as a point of departure.

Much else has been written, of course, on the idea of respect for personal autonomy. Let me give some important examples.

Jonathan Glover, for one, defends the idea that respect for personal autonomy is of value in itself (to the person being respected). This view is put forward most clearly in his book *Causing Death and Saving Lives* (1977).

Other thinkers, such as Robert Nozick, have defended the claim that the individual has an absolute right to have his autonomy protected. Nozick's claim is famously defended in the book, *Anarchy, State, and Utopia* (1974).

Yet other thinkers, such as Immanuel Kant, have defended the idea that there exists an absolute obligation, binding upon all moral agents, to respect the autonomy of other persons.

In 'Against Personal Autonomy' and in Chapter 7 of my book *Hedonistic Utilitarianism* (1998) I have rejected all these claims. In the present context I ignore them. My reason for doing so has already been stated. I do not *need* these speculative ideas in order to arrive at my defence of the principle of respect for the autonomy of the individual in decisions about medical care and social services.

Many modern philosophers have written on the notion of personal autonomy, paternalism and so forth. One original treatment that brings

---

1 In 'The Morality of Clinical Research: A Case Study' (1994) I discuss one of the aforementioned questions, namely, to what extent the patient should be allowed to take responsibility for risks involved in clinical trials.

new clarity to the subject is Gerald Dworkin's 'The Concept of Autonomy' (1981).

An application of the notion in the context of health care, that I have profited from (but disagree with), has already been mentioned. This is Bruce L. Miller's anthologised, 'Autonomy and the Refusal of Lifesaving Treatment' (1981). Others can be found in standard text books in medical ethics, such as Tom L. Beauchamp's and James F. Childress's *Principles of Biomedical Ethics*, where Chapter 3 is devoted to a discussion of respect for autonomy in medicine. I will return to their argument.

There exists an extensive sceptical literature about coercion in relation to psychiatric care. A problem with this literature, from the point of view of the present study, however, is that it is sceptical of psychiatry *as such*. The main thrust of the argument in this literature is that psychiatry, especially to the extent that it takes the form of administration of drugs, is humbug or worse, so people should not be coercively submitted to its putative cures. Some authors, such as Laing even go so far as to deny that there is such a thing as mental illness. There is something wrong, it is claimed, not with the supposedly mentally ill person, but with society.

There are also critics of the entire medical system, such as Illich, who conceive of it as merely ideological machinery, designed to discipline people, not to prevent or cure diseases. These critics too tend to be sceptical, of course, and to be very sceptical indeed, when it comes to *coercive* care.

Now, I do not say that all this is wrong. The problem is, however, that *if* it is wrong, or, at least, if it will eventually come to be seen as very exaggerated, this line of argument against compulsory care vanishes into thin air. So, once again, this is a kind of literature I have largely ignored. There are no references to thinkers such as Laing and Illich in this book. I do return to the question of controversial therapies within psychiatry, however, when I discuss compulsory treatment of mentally ill persons.

An important aspect of my argument are facts about Western law, regulating the use of coercion in care. I have gathered these facts from many sources, specified when I make references to them.

There are also some *general* sources; in particular, I have relied on H.J.J. Leenen *et al.*, *The Rights of Patients in Europe* (1993) and Tor Sverne, 'Comments on the Legislation Concerning Impaired Capacity and Decision-Making in the Health Care Field in England and Wales, the Netherlands, Spain, and Sweden' (1997). A general source about mental health legislation in Europe has been Knud Jensen, 'Mental Health Legislation in Europe' (1994). A general source about legislative responses to HIV/AIDS has been Jonathan M. Mann and Sev S. Fluss, *Legislative Responses to AIDS* (1989). A general source on psychiatry has been James C. Beck, 'Forensic Psychiatry in the USA and the UK: A Clinician's View' (1996). And finally, a general source about reproductive medicine is

C. MacKellar's *Reproductive Medicine and Embryological Research* (1997), which gives an account of the European situation with respect to bioethical legislation.

The aim of this book

The aim of this book can be stated thus. Having outlined the principle of respect for the autonomy of the individual in decisions about medical care and social services, based on the ideal of judicial security and the ideal of anti-paternalism, I look at existing kinds of legislation, regulating the use of coercion in health care and the social services, mainly in Western states, in Europe, the US, Australia, Canada and Japan.

I discuss laws regulating coercion in relation to somatic health care, preventive health care, infectious disease, mental illness, forensic psychiatry, foetal/maternal conflicts and the social services. I argue that, to the extent that such laws do not live up to the principle of respect for the autonomy of the individual in decisions about medical care and social services, flouting either the ideal of judicial security or the ideal of anti-paternalism (or both), the laws should be revised.

Another way of putting the same point, in a less presumptuous manner, would be as follows. In this book I state my principle of respect for the autonomy of the individual in decisions about medical care and social services, I show how it can be vindicated with reference to an anti-paternalistic ideal and the ideal of judicial security, I confront it with existing laws, and, when I find that a certain law conflicts with the principle, I try to find out whether the law or the principle ought to yield.

My *hypothesis* is that the principle should be upheld (and laws in conflict with it yield). My hypothesis is that, if the principle is honoured, we will have a *better* system of health care and social services than if the principle is flouted.

To the extent that the reader shares my belief in the ideals of anti-paternalism and judicial security, he or she should not find this very surprising. One could perhaps say that, if these ideals are taken for granted, then a strong presumption already exists for the plausibility of the principle of respect for the autonomy of the individual in decisions about medical care and social services. However, since I do not want to rely on any speculative values, but on simple utilitarian reasons, this presumption cannot be accepted on its face value. My hypothesis is an *empirical* one.

To put it even less presumptuously, I *conjecture* that, on the whole, more lives will be saved, less harm done and so forth, if we stick to the principle of respect for the autonomy of the individual in decisions about medical care and social services than if we don't.

Of course, in the present context this conjecture cannot be vindicated or conclusively confirmed. If it be vindicated at all, it must vindicated in a piecemeal manner, after a thorough examination of each part of the health care field. This would take many books to achieve.

My treatment of the subject is quite extensive. I do hope to start a discussion, but I also want to confute *some* considerations commonly thought to weigh against the plausibility of my conjecture, and to present *some* strong considerations in favour of it.

2

SOMATIC HEALTH CARE

In ordinary somatic health care circumstances, in all Western countries, the adult individual, who is capable of making an autonomous choice, is granted an absolute veto against treatment; he or she is allowed an absolute right to reject whatever kind of somatic treatment he or she may need. A grown-up patient, for example, who has a vital interest in having a blood transfusion is allowed to abstain from the transfusion, for whatever reasons he or she may have. The doctor may consider the reasons very poor. Yet, for all that, the doctor has to accept the decision made by the patient. The patient has a right to *die* from his or her illness. In the US there is even a federal law to this effect. On 1 December 1991 the Patient Self-Determination Act – a federal law known as the PSDA – went into effect in the United States. It was the first federal legislation regarding life-sustaining treatments (and advance directives, to which I will return).

The situation is different in Japan, of course. Not only do physicians have great authority with respect to the patient, but the autonomy of the patient is restricted also by considerations regarding his or her family. According to Kzumasa Hoshino:

> Japanese people are not accustomed to making medical decisions regarding their own diseases by themselves without consulting the family. This is because of their deep regard and respect for the opinions and feelings of the family. When one member of the family becomes sick, it is the responsibility of the entire family to look after him. . . . The family knows that the care of the sick member is a family matter.
>
> (1996: 17–19)

The Western right of the patient to a veto is guaranteed in the constitution of several European countries. In other European countries it is stated in special health care laws. Moreover, both in the European Convention and, more clearly, in the Convention, worked out by European countries in cooperation with the US and Australia, Canada and Japan, this right is guaranteed, which may make for difficulties in Japan. In Article 5 of the Convention it is stated, as a general rule:

> An intervention in the health field may only be carried out after the person concerned has given free and informed consent to it. This person shall beforehand be given appropriate information as to the purpose and nature of the intervention as well as on its consequences and risks. The person concerned may freely withdraw consent at any time.

Of course, in all countries, a patient who is unconscious when admitted to an intensive care unit will be treated without having previously given consent. If necessary, the patient will be operated on or given blood transfusions and so on, if this is considered to be in their best interests. In the circumstances, it is simply taken for granted that this is what the patient wants. This is taken care of in Article 8 of the Convention:

> When because of an emergency situation the appropriate consent cannot be obtained, any medically necessary intervention may be carried out immediately for the benefit of the health of the individual concerned.

However, if the patient wakes up from the coma and states that he or she does not want any continued treatment, or not continued treatment of a certain kind (such as blood transfusions), and if he or she is capable of reaching a decision (he or she is not confused because of the illness), and he or she is informed as to the consequences of refusal, his or her 'no' will be taken for an answer, even if it means that the patient, who could have been cured, will die.

In the present chapter, I will discuss whether this absolute right to a veto of any kind of treatment for somatic illness, granted to adult patients, is acceptable. I will also discuss whether it should be extended to a right to a parental veto of medical treatment of one's children.

Having settled these two quite straightforward questions I will move on to cover two areas where things are less straightforward: how is society to react to people who try to commit suicide and how is society to react when patients suffering from senile dementia, or mental impairment, refuse treatment for somatic diseases?

An absolute right to a veto

Is the absolute right to a veto of any kind of treatment for somatic illness, granted to adult patients in the EU, the US, Canada and Australia (but not Japan), acceptable? I think it is.

Should this right be extended also to a right for parents to prevent their children being treated as the doctor sees fit? To some extent it should, but there is a certain limit to this right, to be specified below. This limit is, one way or another, respected in all Western countries.

The argument for an absolute right to a veto of any kind of treatment for somatic illness granted to adult patients is straightforward. It is based on the necessity of all potential patients being able to trust the medical system. Unless this right is granted to all potential patients, some patients, with certain religious beliefs, such as Jehovah's Witnesses, for example, would never dare to consult the medical profession. It is likely that this would mean that more people would die unnecessarily from curable diseases (because they would not get the care they need), as compared to the actual situation, where people very *rarely* die from curable diseases (because they reject vital treatments).

Moreover, and perhaps even more important, unless this right is granted to all potential patients, many people would lack the security it means to know that, if one needs to visit a doctor, one can do so, and receive whatever treatment there may be for one's illness, on terms acceptable to oneself.

It might be tempting to argue that, if the patient's decision is based on a firm conviction, if it truly represents the patient's will and so forth, it should be respected. However, if it is the result of poor reasoning, or if it is based on a decision that is not 'genuinely' the wish of the patient, it need not be respected. In the latter case, it may be overruled, in the best interest of the patient, by sound medical reasoning. As was noted in Chapter 1, this is what has been argued by, for example, Bruce L. Miller (1981).

Miller describes situations where patients have been coercively treated in a life-saving manner. Some such cases are acceptable to Miller. He thinks precisely of situations where the patient's decision to refuse treatment is based on poor reasoning, or where it is based on a decision that is not genuinely the patient's 'own'. On my interpretation of him, his argument is that a patient's right to refuse treatment should only exist when, roughly speaking, the patient has *actually* exercised his or her capacity for autonomous decision-making (roughly as defined in Chapter 1). Is this line of argument acceptable?

We should resist this line of argument. The reason for doing so is that it makes the patient's right to a veto much too weak.

I concede that if the patient has not reached an autonomous decision because he or she is not *capable* of doing so (because of, say, mental illness), then we may exercise his or her right on his or her behalf, treating the patient as we see fit, in his or her own best interest. When doing so we act on the presumption that this is what the patient would have decided, had she or he been capable of reaching an autonomous decision. However, if the reason that the patient did not reach an autonomous decision was that he or she *did not bother* to try to do so, or *did not want* to do so, then we should not coerce the patient.

There are many critical situations in life, outside the scope of the health care system, where we refuse to make autonomous decisions. We put our lives in jeopardy and we simply refuse to consider any arguments intended to point this out to us. In the circumstances, it may be appropriate for some authorities to *urge* us to reconsider the case, but it is not appropriate for them to *coerce* us. So patients should not be coerced in similar situations.

In some situations it is impossible to *tell* whether the patient's refusal to take an autonomous decision is due to lack of a capacity or a will to do so. Then it is appropriate to coerce the patient, in the hope and in the expectation that the decision reached on his or her behalf will come eventually to be endorsed also by the patient.

This is not controversial, I assume. Miller gives a good example of this. A 38-year-old man with mild upper respiratory infection suddenly developed severe headache, stiff neck and high fever. He went to an emergency room for help. The diagnosis was pneumococcal meningitis, a bacterial meningitis almost always fatal if not treated. If treatment is delayed, permanent neurological damage is likely. A physician told the patient that urgent treatment was needed to save his life and forestall brain damage. The patient refused to consent to treatment saying that he wanted to be allowed to die.[1] In the circumstances, the possibility could not be ruled out that the meningitis had made the patient incompetent. He could (and should) therefore be coercively treated.

However, if we are convinced that the patient is capable of reaching an autonomous decision (the patient is grown up, suffers from no known mental illness, has been able so far to care for him or herself, has no somatic disease that may impair his or her judgement, and so forth), then his or her 'no' should be taken for an answer, no matter how imprudent the decision may seem to us. After all, the patient *does* have a privileged epistemological position, and a very special interest, *vis-à-vis* his or her own case.

Again, an example discussed by Miller may be of interest. A 52-year-old married man was admitted to a medical intensive care unit after a suicide attempt. He had retired two years earlier because of progressive physical disability related to multiple sclerosis during the fifteen years before admission. He had successfully adapted to his physical limitations, remaining actively involved in family matters with his wife and two teenage sons. However, during the three months before admission, he had become morose and withdrawn. On the evening of admission, while alone, he had ingested an unknown quantity of diazepam. When his family returned six

---

1 The example stems originally from Eric J. Cassell, 'The Function of Medicine' (1976).

hours later, they found the patient semi-conscious. He had left a suicide note. On admission, physical examination showed several neurological deficits, but no more severe than in recent examinations. The patient was alert and fully able to converse. He expressed to the house officers his strong belief in a patient's right to die with dignity. He stressed the 'meaningless' aspects of his life related to his loss of function, insisting that he did not want vigorous medical intervention should serious complications develop.

So far it seemed appropriate to concede to his demand. However, a consultation with members of the psychiatric liaison service was requested. During the initial consultation the patient showed that the onset of his withdrawal and depression coincided with a diagnosis of inoperable cancer in his mother-in-law, who lived in another city. His wife had spent more and more time satisfying her mother's needs. In fact, on the night of his suicide attempt, the patient's wife and two sons had left him alone for the first time to visit his mother-in-law.[2]

This further piece of information should give us pause, according to Miller, who is now prepared to argue that the wish to die, expressed by the patient, may not have been genuinely his own. So it was not imperative for the doctors to honour it, according to Miller. And there is an 'outcome' of the story, which is supposed to substantiate Miller's conclusion. This is how the 'happy ending' goes.

The patient had too much pride to complain to his wife about his feelings of abandonment. He was able to recognise that his suicide attempt and his insistence on death with dignity were attempts to draw the family's attention to his needs. Discussion with all four family members led to improved communication and acknowledgement of the patient's special emotional needs. After these conversations, the patient explicitly retracted both his suicide threats and his demand that no supportive medical efforts be undertaken.

What does this show us? Nothing at all, as far as *I* can see. To be sure, the patient should have a right to consult a psychiatrist and to change his mind about his decision. However, the fact that eventually he *did* change his mind does not show that the original decision should not have been followed.

Again, in the first place, the original desire may be the more genuine one, the other one being the result of manipulation. Who are we to tell, even if we are psychiatrists? After all, the patient was mentally healthy; no psychiatric *diagnosis* was in place in the example.

Second, and more importantly, unless *each* judgement made by the patient, the original one as well as the revised one, be respected, at the

2 This example originates from David L. Jackson and Stuart Youngner, 'Patient Autonomy and "Death with Dignity"' (1979: 406).

time when it is made, there is no possibility for a patient in a situation like this to feel *secure* in relation to medical authorities.

To conclude: unless the right of the patient to have his or her autonomy respected includes a right to argue in a rash manner and to act from interests that are less than 'genuinely one's own', the right will be of little interest to the patient.

Unless the right includes a right to poor reasoning and the right to act out of interests that are poorly integrated with one's 'true' personality, it will always and only too easily be overruled, as soon as a patient has reached, by the lights of the doctor, an imprudent decision.

Unless the patient's right to a veto against treatment includes a right to poor reasoning and to reasoning based on 'false' (in contradistinction to 'true') interests, it will not provide people in general with the sense of security they need in their relation to the medical profession; after all, we all know that, one day, *qua* patients, most of us will have to meet with this profession, perhaps in a matter of life and death.

The parents' right to decide for their children

While the argument why adult patients, capable of making an autonomous decision, should be granted an absolute veto against medical (somatic) care is straightforward and a matter of trust, the argument why this right to an absolute veto should not be extended to parents, on behalf of their children, is less straightforward.

To be sure, in normal circumstances, the parents must be allowed to make medical choices on behalf of their children. However, there is a limit to this right This right cannot be absolute.

Again it can be said that, unless the right to an absolute veto is extended to parents, on behalf of their children, some parents, who for religious reasons, say, oppose certain standard treatments, will hesitate to seek medical advice on behalf of their children. This would be a very strong argument indeed for a parental right to decide for their children; it would mean that unless the parental veto was respected, many children would not receive *any* kind of medical care.

However, many social practices, at least in most European countries, make it *impossible* for parents to keep their children outside the health care system. So, in most cases, the children *will* receive treatment when they need it, irrespective of the will of their parents. They will receive it through the intervention of the doctors supervising the maternal care centres, the nursery day care centres, the public school system and so forth. Moreover, in some cases, parents who belong to religions forbidding medical intervention on behalf of their children seek help in order to escape responsibility for the situation themselves. They cannot consent to treatment of their children, but they can live with the fact if such treatment is imposed on their children, leaving them without any responsibility for this.

All this means that the argument from trust, which is so strong in relation to adult persons, does not count so strongly in defence of a right to an absolute *parental* veto (on behalf of one's children) against medical measures.

The parents may protest, of course, when the doctors want to operate on their child, or when they want to give blood transfusions to their child. And the parents' right to a veto ought not to be given up too easily. However, when parents use their veto, it is of the utmost importance that the doctors (and nurses) try to convince the parents that the treatment is medically necessary.

Some religious advice may be well placed too. The parents may have argued incorrectly from their own religious premisses. It might be acceptable to them, for example, when the doctor gives blood to the child, if they are not *themselves* involved in the transaction. Some religious authority they respect may be consulted and asked to point this out to them.

But, of course, the parents may persist in their insistence that the child should not be treated. Then, if the life and health of the child are put in jeopardy, society should act. This is allowed for by the law in all European countries. However, there are three different ways in which society can take action.

In some European countries, consent by the legal guardian, such as the two parents together, can be replaced by a decision by a court. This is the case, for example, in Austria, Belgium and France (Leenen *et al* 1993: 99–101).

In other countries, when the life of the child is at stake, the law gives the doctor the right to act contrary to the will of the parents. This is the case in Greece where, for example, blood transfusions can be given to children belonging to the Jehovah's Witnesses.

On a third model, practised in Finland, Sweden and the Netherlands (Leenen *et al.* 1993: 101–104), it is possible for a court to appoint a trustee for the child, if there is a conflict of interest between the guardian and the child. In situations, for example, in which the parent of an under-age child refuses to allow the treatment necessary to ward off a serious threat to life or health, measures are taken to remove the child from the care of that parent and to place the child in the custody of something like a Child Welfare Board.

Which one of these possible models is preferable? I feel a slight inclination towards the third model. In normal circumstances, society should not meddle with the decisions taken by the parents on behalf of the child. In normal circumstances the parents should be able to approach the health care system without any fear that their views about the interest of the child will not be honoured. No court should intervene in the process.

Neither should there be room for the doctors to exercise any kind of licence.

However, in *extreme* cases, some kind of action *must* be taken by society. Then it should be taken in accordance with the third model. A Child Welfare Board should take over the custody of the child from the parents for a limited time. The child is then treated for the disease and, when cured, given back to the custody of the parents.

The main argument for this tactic is that this is in line with the way society protects the interests of children *in general*, when there is a conflict of interest between parents and children. So this possibility of a take-over of responsibility from society in medical contexts should not be viewed as any *special* threat to parental authority.

In extreme situations, when, after having been treated, the child is given back to the custody of the parents, they may come to reject the child altogether. They may consider the child doomed to hell and they may want to have nothing more to do with the child. In that case, society must make preparations for foster parents to take over the responsibility for the child, with the aim of having the child eventually adopted.

But could it not be plausibly argued, against all the three models practised in European countries, that the parents have a *right* to care for their children? I think not, if this putative right is taken as a *moral premiss*. It is hard to believe that, as a matter of moral principle, *any* person has a right to take decisions on behalf of *anyone else*. If, as a matter of moral principle, there are human rights at all, they should safeguard the individual *against* the intervention of other agents. It is not plausible that, as a matter of moral principle, there exists a right to property, including human beings. Parents do not *own* their children.

Of course, it could be argued that through an act of law, parents should be granted the judicial right to take all kinds of medical decisions on behalf of their children. It could be argued that this is what follows from sound moral principles together with a correct statement of relevant facts. However, in the foregoing argument, this is exactly what I have been denying.

It may be sound social policy to allow parents a veto on behalf of their children, as long as they have custody of their children (society should not, in normal circumstances, meddle with the decisions taken by the parents). However, such an absolute veto can be misused. There comes a point, when this is actually the case, where society must take the custody of the child from the parents, in the best interests of the child.

To be sure, there are some arguments against such a proposal but there are also arguments for it. And, in the present context, the latter must be given most weight.

It should be noted, however, that the system here adumbrated, and practised in many countries, is not ideal. There *are* important drawbacks associated with it. In particular, the system does not allow that *all* parents have *complete* confidence in the health care system. It does not provide all parents with incentives to see to it that their children are always provided with the medical care they may actually need. In extreme cases, it may mean that some parents hide their children from the medical authorities, putting the lives of their children unnecessarily in jeopardy.

However, the bad side-effects of a system granting the parents an absolute veto on behalf of their children in medical affairs are *worse* than the bad side-effects of a system that does not grant them this absolute veto.

A system granting the parents an absolute veto might mean, in some circumstances, that children already in the hands of the medical authorities, children who could be saved by medical intervention, would be sacrificed. This is not acceptable, either in the particular case, or as social policy. Most people would find it difficult to live with such a system and with the knowledge that children were sacrificed in this manner; they would resent the way that children could be sacrificed for religious reasons that most people do not understand or do not sympathise with.

Furthermore, there are strong considerations of judicial security underwriting the appropriateness of the actual practice of treating children against the will of their parents. For in *other* situations, where parents cannot, or simply are not, prepared to provide for the needs of their children, society does not, and should not, dare to take over custody of the children. But there is no good reason for society to treat *medical* needs any differently than it treats *other* needs of the children.

Could children decide for themselves?

I have argued that, in normal circumstances, parents should be allowed, in their dealings with medical authorities, to exercise a parental veto on behalf of their children. However, there is a limit to this right. Custody of the child should be taken from the parents, if they exercise their right to a veto in a manner that threatens the life or health of their child.

Where does all this leave the children themselves? Should they not have any say? I do believe that they should have a 'say'. Both medical authorities and parents should be encouraged to take the opinion of the children into account. Children should be educated to take responsibility for their lives. They should be encouraged to voice their opinion.

Actually, there is a growing recognition that a minor who is capable of judging the situation and making up his or her mind on treatment decisions should be enabled to express his or her opinion. In Article 5, paragraph 2, of the Convention, minors in Europe, in the US, Canada, and in Australia and Japan, are granted this right: 'The opinion of the minor shall be taken into consideration as an increasingly determining factor in proportion to his or her age and degree of maturity.'

In Finland, France, Luxembourg, the Netherlands and Norway, the law requires that health care practitioners take account of the view of such minors. However, there is no uniformity on the age at which a partial capability to participate in health care decisions is recognised. Various ages are specified (12, 13, 14 or 15 years) (Leenen *et al.* 1993: 129).

This vagueness, of course, reflects the fact that the maturing of a child is a process which can develop in many different ways. So it is not possible to stipulate any *absolute* rights to a decision of one's own, valid for children at various ages.

In acts of law various age limits could be set for when the child has a right to voice an opinion, and so forth. However, when there is a sharp conflict of interest, the ultimate authority must lie elsewhere.

In normal circumstances, I have argued, ultimate authority should lie with the parents. And in very special circumstances, when custody of the child has been taken from the parents, ultimate authority must lie with society.

There are some exceptions to this, however. One relates to abortion, the other to donation of organs for transplantation.

The right to abortion should always lie with the pregnant woman, it seems to me. In Chapter 7 I will state my arguments for this view. Now, if this is true in general, it must also be true for pregnant women who are themselves children. Their right to abortion should be honoured by society, irrespective of the will of their parents. After all, these young women, and not their parents, are to live with the life-long consequences of their decision to carry, or not to carry, their pregnancy to term.

It seems wise to grant children an absolute right to a veto also when it comes to donating some organ for transplantation. In particular, such a right should be honoured when there is a definite risk involved in the transaction, a risk that the donor will be hurt somehow. To sneak organs from a child, even with the informed consent of its parents, and for the benefit of a brother or sister of the child, is not acceptable. Once again, an argument from trust speaks very clearly in this direction. Children in general may come to fear both parents and medical authorities, if, in their dealings with them, they feel that they are not granted a right to physical integrity.

Suicide

Even if, in most Western countries, grown-up patients capable of taking an autonomous decision have a right to abstain from medical treatment, an exception is made when it comes to patients who try, or have tried, to commit suicide. The standard approach from medical authorities to such patients is to stop them, if possible, from committing suicide and always to try to resuscitate these patients.

31

It is true that in one place in the world (the Northern Territory in Australia) people had for a while (before the euthanasia law enacted in this state was overturned by the federal parliament) and under certain circumstances, a right to medical assistance (or euthanasia) when they wanted to take their lives. Moreover, in the Netherlands, some patients are given a similar kind of assistance (as a concession by the doctor, not as a patient's right). And in Switzerland medically assisted suicide has been legal, and regularly practised, although little publicised, for many years. A discussion is taking place in the US about the establishment of a system of physician-assisted suicide for terminally ill patients. However, even in the Northern Territory in Australia, in Switzerland and in the Netherlands, the *standard* approach to people who have tried to commit suicide has been always to treat them aggressively. This is also the case in Oregon, where the physician-assisted suicide law (Measure 16, passed in 1994) has been recently put into practice. Physician-assisted suicide is the exception, thoroughly regulated by law, not the rule.

Is this practice of aggressive treatment of people who have tried to commit suicide compatible with the principle of respect for the patient's autonomy? Obviously, it is not. Yet, for all that, the rationale behind the standard practice is rather obvious and sound. The rationale is as follows.

It takes time to ascertain whether an individual who tries to commit suicide, or who has tried to commit suicide, is competent. So, whether the doctor tries to stop the patient from committing suicide (or resuscitates the patient) or not, there is a positive risk that harm is being done to the patient. However, in most cases, it is *less* serious to save the life of a person who should have been allowed to commit suicide than not to save a person, who should have been helped to continued life.

Even if it may seem cynical, there is some truth in the saying that the person who had good reasons to commit suicide, but who was stopped from doing so, could often make a second attempt. But there is never any second possibility open to the person who committed suicide, but who should have been stopped from doing so (who could not make an autonomous decision as to whether he or she should live or not).

Now, even if a sound rationale exists behind the widespread medical practice of trying to stop people from committing suicide, and of aggressively treating those who have tried in vain to take their lives, it is troublesome that this practice means that patients who have good reasons to commit suicide are sometimes stopped from doing so, or hindered in their attempts so that they must perhaps make repeated attempts before they succeed. It is tempting to try to see whether there is some way of honouring both the autonomy of the patients and of retaining a practice where people who have failed in their attempts to take their lives are aggressively treated.

At least a *logical* possibility exists of satisfying both these demands. The possibility lies in a more liberal view of medically assisted (planned) suicides. I will discuss this possibility without taking any firm stance towards it. I have not been able to make up my mind definitely concerning the *pros* and *cons* in this context. In particular, much empirical evidence is wanting.

Before going into my somewhat radical proposal, however, I need to say something more about how I intend to define the notion of suicide.

The notion of suicide

What does it mean for a person to commit suicide? The notion is sometimes, as with Durkheim, defined in a very inclusive manner; the notion is taken to apply as soon as someone has done something, actively or passively, which brought about the death of the agent, and which he or she knew could lead to death. This means that both Jesus and Socrates committed 'suicide'. However, I would like to use the term in a more restricted sense.

To be sure, we can bring about our own death both actively (such as when we shoot or hang ourselves) or passively (such as when we decide to stay on the tracks when we see a train approaching). However, in order for our bringing our own death about to count as 'suicide', we must *want* our own death (not simply foresee it), we must *seek* it for its own sake (in some rare cases) or (in general) as a means to some goal.

If a person decides not to accept to have his leg amputated (in spite of his or her developing gangrene), foresees that this will lead to death and dies as a consequence of his or her rejection of the treatment, then this is a case of 'suicide', in Durkheim's sense of the word, but not in my sense.[3] At least this is the case if, as in the circumstances it is natural to assume, death is not actively sought by the patient; death is sought neither for its own sake nor as a means to any end. It is reasonable to assume that, if this patient could retain life *and* the infected limb, this patient would do so.

Note, however, that, even on my restrictive use of the word 'suicide', a person who voluntarily starves him- or herself to death *does* commit suicide.

This means that there exists an important exception to my statement above that people are not in general allowed to commit medically assisted suicide. In most European countries, in the US and in Australia and Canada, people *are* allowed to starve themselves to death, even in hospitals, and they have a right to good care and nursing while dying. This

3 This is how Durkheim, in *Le Suicide*, defines the notion: 'On appelle suicide tout cas de mort qui resulte directement ou indirectement d'un acte positif ou negatif, accompli par la victime elle-même et qu'elle savait devoir produire ce resultat' (1930: 5).

is true even in England and Wales, where suicide is no longer a crime, but where aiding and abetting suicide is. Inconsistently enough, a doctor would not be guilty of aiding and abetting a suicide by adhering to a patient's wishes in relation to feeding or other treatment.

A radical proposal

A way of reconciling the medical practice of aggressively treating people who have tried to commit suicide with the principle of respect for the autonomy of the patients, as I have indicated, would be to adopt a more liberal medical stance towards planned suicides. If a liberal medical stance is taken towards planned suicides, then the practice of aggressively treating people who have impulsively tried to commit suicide becomes less repugnant. The most thoroughgoing reconciliatory approach would be as follows.[4]

We would develop a system of suicide clinics. The main objective of these clinics would be to prevent suicide by rendering suicide unnecessary. People who approached the clinic would be offered help with the problems leading to their desire to die. If they suffered from depression they would be offered anti-depressant treatment and psychotherapy. If they had financial problems they would be offered economic help. If they suffered from somatic disease, they would be offered the best available cures or, if cure was out of question, good palliative care. However, if the patient was a grown-up, capable of reaching an autonomous decision, who has tried anti-depressant treatment (if that was medically indicated) and persists in wanting to die, then, as a last resort, reluctantly and sadly, the patient would be offered medical assistance in his or her suicide (which could take place where the patient saw fit, in his or her home, for example).

Ought an examination by a psychiatrist be mandatory at the clinic, before a wish to die is honoured? I think not. The clinic must have psychiatric expertise at its disposal, of course, and the physicians at the clinic might refer a patient to a psychiatrist. However, there is no use psychiatrists trying to decide in general whether a patient is capable of making an autonomous decision or not. This is not a medical decision at all. Psychiatrists are no better trained for it than other persons (doctors). This has been persuasively argued by, among others, Stuart J. Youngner.[5]

However, when a physician feels that a suicidal candidate may suffer from mental illness, making him or her incapable of reaching an autono-

---

4 The idea is not new. It was discussed, for example, in France back in 1919 when a Dr Binet-Sangle proposed that 'suicide centres' be established (Binet-Sangle 1919: 107–152).
5 For example, in his speech to the III World Bioethics Congress in San Francisco 1996, with the title, 'Please Don't Make Psychiatrists the Gatekeepers for Physician-Assisted Suicide'.

mous decision, then the physician should refer the patient to a psychiatrist for consultation and a proper diagnosis. If it turns out that the patient does suffer from a kind of mental disorder, which makes him or her incapable of taking an autonomous decision, then he or she cannot be granted the right to die with medical assistance at the clinic.

This does not mean that mentally ill persons may not in some circumstances have a right to die. In some circumstances mentally ill persons *are* capable of reaching an autonomous decision (for example, when such a person is not in an acute psychotic state). However, if, being psychotic, they are not capable of making an autonomous decision, their case belongs to the more general problem of euthanasia, which will not be discussed in the present book.

It is clear, it seems to me, that if suicide clinics are in operation, then there is no problem in continuing the practice of aggressively treating at intensive care units people who have impulsively tried in vain to take their lives.

In this, it should be noted, my proposal, while radical indeed, even in the context of the US discussion about physician-assisted suicide for terminally ill patients, is much less radical than the views propagated by Thomas Szasz (1986), who rejects the very idea that suicide is a mental health problem, that mental health practitioners and institutions have a professional duty to try to prevent it, and that it is a legitimate function of the state to empower such professionals and institutions (especially psychiatrists and psychiatric institutions) to impose coercive interventions on persons diagnosed as posing a suicidal risk.

Why would it be right aggressively to treat those who have impulsively tried to take their lives? Well, if these people had been serious in their attempts, they could have approached a suicide clinic! Since they did not do so, it is only natural to assume that they did not really want to die, and this assumption should not be taken as in any way offensive. The *assumption* is based on a very reasonable *pre*sumption.

Would it be wise to develop a system of suicide clinics? I have indicated that I am not sure. However, if three important conditions were satisfied, I *would* be prepared to argue in their defence. These three conditions are as follows. First, the clinics must be an effective means to the prevention of rash and irrational suicides. Second, the clinics must be a good alternative for persons who have good reasons to commit suicide. Third, the existence of the clinics should not lead, on balance, to bad and untended side-effects. Could these conditions be met? I will discuss them in order.

The prevention of tragic suicide

It seems to be part of the received opinion that many suicides, perhaps most suicides, are irrational. And it is often taken for granted that this is even more true of *attempts* at suicide. There are very few rational suicide attempts, it has been maintained.[6] But if this is so, it may be argued, the introduction of suicide clinics would be dangerous.

The introduction of the clinics could mean that *many* people who have no good reasons to kill themselves would do so. More people would kill themselves, with the help of the clinics, than today kill themselves on their own. After all, it takes *courage* to commit suicide on one's own. Your attempt on your own to kill yourself may fail, you may cause yourself pain, and loss of dignity. The clinic could guarantee success, dignity and painlessness. This argument is far from convincing. It could be questioned on at least two counts.

First, it is not at all *obvious* that most suicides are irrational. After all, in order to be 'rational' (this is how I use the term, at any rate) the suicidal act must be consistent with the desires and beliefs of the person who commits it. It is not very far-fetched to assume that this is often the case. But this means that there are *many* rational suicides. Note that, if this were not so, then most suicidal acts could not be rationally explained. This is hardly plausible.

Perhaps we should introduce, in addition to the notion of a rational suicide, a stronger notion of a philosophical suicide. A philosophical suicide is not only rational, in the light of the agent's actual desires and beliefs, but the desires of this person are resistant to cognitive psycho-therapy (i.e. even if the person becomes aware of why he or she entertains them, they do not go away), and the beliefs the person entertains have been formed through mechanisms that are, in general, reliable.[7]

A suicide that is not in this sense 'philosophical' I will call a 'tragic' suicide.

Even so it is far from clear that many suicides are not both rational and philosophical. After all, many clever and influential philosophers, from Schopenhauer onwards, have actually *argued* that life is less important than we often believe.

In many situations, people refrain from suicide, not because they have good reasons to do so, but because they are in the grips of sentiments, selected for by evolution, to be sure, but yet, for all that, sentiments detrimental to a *good* life, these philosophers argue.

If these philosophers are right, then it is not far-fetched to assume that those who are prepared to give up their lives may have very good reasons to do so. Their suicides are far from tragic. In many cases, these philosophers would add, we who *don't* commit suicide may be the ones who

6 See, for example, George E. Murphy 'Suicide and the Right to Die' (1973). I have myself often met this reaction from Swedish psychiatrists when discussing suicide with them.
7 This comes close to an idea expressed and defended by the moral philosopher Richard Brandt in *A Theory of the Good and the Right* (1979).

(because of cowardice, for example) cannot face up to the realities of life. We may then need the aid of the clinics to do so.

Second, even if most actual suicides are tragic and very few actual suicides are rational or philosophical, it is not at all obvious that the introduction of the clinics would mean an increase in the number of unnecessary and tragic suicides. To be sure, if we have a system of suicide clinics, then *some* people will unnecessarily kill themselves, with the help of the clinic. These people could have led good lives, on the whole, if they had held on to life in their situation of crisis, and some of them, at least, would have done so, if they had not been offered any help from the clinic.

However, it is not very far-fetched to assume that there are also many cases where people do kill themselves, without any assistance from the medical system, where these people would have held on to life, if only they had been offered appropriate help. And it is not very far-fetched to assume that a suicide clinic was really what these people needed.

How can a suicide clinic help a person to go on living? The person may need a place to go to where his or her desire to commit suicide is taken seriously (and not as a symptom of mental illness).

Few people who actually succeed in their attempts to commit suicide have received adequate treatment for their problems. For example, very few depressed people who kill themselves have used anti-depressant treatment.[8] It seems as though traditional psychiatry is not capable of reaching these patients. This may be due to a lack of basic trust, on the part of these patients, in their relation to psychiatry. The suicide clinic may be a way of restoring confidence.

Could the clinic provide a good alternative?

Let us now focus on the cases where an individual has a good reason to commit suicide.

Consider a person who suffers from an incurable disease. He may want to kill himself, after having made necessary preparations, after having said good-bye to those who are near and dear, and so forth. Or he may be a solitary individual, suffering from a severe mental disorder, being, for a moment, competent to reach an autonomous decision (before the disorder makes him incompetent once more). It seems obvious to me that these persons could be helped by the existence of a suicide clinic. The clinic would mean that they could kill themselves, without fear of failure, pain or lack of dignity.

I take it for granted that the former person could be assisted, when the time comes, in his home, if this is what he wants. Perhaps this person wants, not primarily, assistance in killing himself, but control. He needs to

---

8 This seems to be the case in Sweden, at any rate (see Isacsson *et al.* 1994).

know that, if things become too hard, there is an option open to him. As a matter of fact, it is quite possible that he will not use the opportunity to kill himself. Eventually he may come to prefer to live through to a natural death than kill himself, and he may dare to take this option in the secure conviction that, if things turn worse, he can obtain help in killing himself.

Or the person may want simply to walk to the clinic and, without much ado, finish her life. In the circumstances, to most of us this kind of end would be much preferable to our throwing ourselves under a train, or hanging or poisoning ourselves. Moreover, this planned and medically assisted death of ours, should it turn out to be necessary, would be far preferable to third parties, who need not run us down with the trains they drive, or find us hanging where they did not expect to, and so forth. It would also render *euthanasia* unnecessary in the circumstances.

Side-effects

So far I have concentrated on possible *direct* effects of a system of suicide clinics. However, much of the discussion of assisted suicide, as well as of euthanasia, has been focused on possible side-effects of the practice. There are positive as well as negative possible side-effects of a system of suicide clinics.

On the positive side we must reckon with the sense of security we can all feel that, if things were to come to the worst, and if we came to have good reasons to kill ourselves, there would be a way of doing so, not presupposing unusual courage, to wit, a way of guaranteeing success, painlessness and dignity. This seems to me to be of great importance.

On the negative side we must reckon with the possible *uneasiness* people may come to feel that, if they become a burden to society or their relatives, they would be coerced, manipulated or cajoled into taking their lives. We must also reckon with the possibility that, instead of developing a good and effective *palliative* care, the health care system will offer patients suicide as an alternative. Clinics may become a means to saving scarce medical resources.

How are we to assess these possibilities? It seems to me that while the positive side-effects are certain, the negative ones are merely speculative. This means that there exists at least a presumption in favour of the clinics, as far as the side-effects go.

To the extent that there is empirical evidence forthcoming, mainly from the Dutch experience of a system of euthanasia and assisted suicide, this seems to be reassuring. The system practised in the Netherlands has, thus far, proved to be stable. It has not meant that the Netherlands have slid down any slippery slope towards barbarism.[9]

9 See the so called Remmelink Report summarised in van der Maas *et al.* (1991) and the report of the study repeating the Remmelink study, van der Maas *et al.* (1996).

However, the empirical data are few, and the Dutch model is in one respect much less radical than the one adumbrated here (you need to suffer intolerably, with no prospect of relief, although the disease need not be terminal, in order to be a candidate for assisted suicide in the Netherlands; in the model here discussed there is no 'need requirement' at all). At the same time, in a different respect, the Dutch model is *more* radical than the one adumbrated here, in that it allows, not only for medically assisted suicide, but for euthanasia as well (which is not supposed to take place at the suicide clinics here discussed).

Now, since euthanasia is beyond the scope of the present book, I will say no more about it here. Judging from the Dutch case, however, it seems safe to conclude that *some* system of active and intentional euthanasia *can* be upheld, without society for that reason deteriorating *very quickly* into something bad and inhumane. And if this is possible with a system of euthanasia it should be possible, as well, with a system of medically assisted *suicide* (where there is no doubt that the patient, who is the one doing the actual killing, consents to the act).

However, it is a far cry from the system I have adumbrated here, where there exists a right to assisted suicide, for all adult and competent patients, to a system more similar to the Dutch model. So it is difficult to generalise from the Dutch example. Crucial evidence is wanting.

Against the medical profession's mission?

It is not possible to tell with any firm conviction whether the three conditions just discussed can be satisfied or not. In particular, the first one, to the effect that a system of suicide clinics would be a good preventive measure (preventing tragic suicides), and the third one, relating to the side-effects, are difficult to assess. I have to leave the problem as unfinished business.

However, it might be argued that even if the three conditions were actually met, it would not be a proper objective for the medical profession to assist in suicides. And, even if it were, it could be maintained, it would not be possible to enrol (any decent) doctors in it. I will have none of this.

Medical codes of various kinds are historic documents. The Hippocratic oath, for example, prohibits abortion. Few modern doctors abide by that requirement. So, even if some medical codes go against any kind of medical assistance in suicide, this should not be taken to settle the matter. We must inquire whether there exists a sound and timely rationale for such requirements.

Now, is there a sound rationale behind the idea that doctors should never assist in suicide? Perhaps there exists such a rationale. If the three requirements discussed above are not met, such a rationale does exist.

But what if these requirements can be met, does there still exist some kind of rationale for a prohibition against doctors assisting people who want to commit suicide? The only plausible candidate for such a prohibition, it seems to me, would be if it could be argued from the Sanctity of Life Doctrine that suicide is morally objectionable *per se*. If it is wrong to *take* one's life, irrespective of the consequences of doing so, then it is probably wrong also to *assist* someone who takes his or her life.

I do not think that any such absolute moral prohibition against suicide exists. Many philosophers share or have shared my view, such as Seneca (1920), Hume (1963), the classical utilitarians and most contemporary philosophers. Quite a few thinkers have argued to the opposite effect, however. Some of them have taken as their point of departure the religious idea that life is a gift from God. So by giving it up, we offend our benefactor. But even if life is a gift from God I find it hard to believe that, if this gift has become a burden to us, we do not have the right to give it up. A *good* God, at any rate, should take no offence if we do.

Other moral critics of suicide have taken as their point of departure the idea that we must never give up our autonomy. This is true, of course, of Immanuel Kant. As has already been noted, I do not share his idea that autonomy is a positive obligation, however. Moreover, none of Kant's arguments to this effect, relating to the question of suicide, is convincing. One argument is that to 'use life for its own destruction, to use life for producing lifelessness, is self-contradictory'. I have not been able to grasp the meaning of this argument. If taken literally it seems to imply that suicide is impossible. However, suicide is clearly a possibility, and suicide is seen, even by Kant, to be a possibility, otherwise he would not have bothered to argue against it.

Another argument put forward by Kant is that suicide is 'abominable' because 'it degrades man's inner worth below that of the animal creation'. This argument follows upon the observation that 'all nature seeks its own preservation'.[10] This is to some extent true, and I suppose there is an evolutionary explanation why we do not easily give up our lives. However, if someone, this fact to the contrary notwithstanding, actually wants to kill him- or herself, then this indicates, it seems to me, that his or her reasons for doing so must be very strong indeed, so I think there is a presumption that we should respect them.

Note also that it is hard to see how Kant's absolute moral rejection of suicide can be defended with reference to his more basic ideas, to wit, his Categorical Imperative. According to the Categorical Imperative, we must be prepared to universalise our moral judgements: 'Act only on that maxim through which you can at the same time will that it should become a universal law' (Kant 1964: 88). However, no one should find it at all

---

10 The quotations are from Immanuel Kant (1963: 148–154).

difficult to accept, as a universal rule, that whenever someone finds that her life has irrevocably lost all kinds of positive value (to herself as well as to anyone else) then she may readily give it up.

Other philosophers yet have just stated, without giving arguments for this position, that suicide is not only morally wrong, but very seriously wrong (most famously, perhaps, Ludwig Wittgenstein). According to Wittgenstein:

> If suicide is allowed then everything is allowed. If anything is not allowed then suicide is not allowed. This throws a light on the nature of ethics, for suicide is, so to speak, the elementary sin.
>
> (1961: 91)

Since Wittgenstein produces no arguments in defence of his position there is little to be said about it. It must suffice to note that his view is a very *cruel* one indeed.

Note, furthermore, that if it *is* argued that suicide is morally wrong as such, and if it *is* conceded that the three requirements discussed above could be met, then we would be facing a genuine dilemma. Doctors would be prohibited by their medical ethics from taking part in a practice that, if it were developed, would effectively prevent more tragic suicides than it would encourage.

Finally, is there any truth in the saying that it would be impossible to enrol decent doctors in a system of suicide clinics? I think not. If it did turn out that, as a matter of fact, the system prevented many tragic suicides, then I think many decent physicians would be willing to work at the clinics.

A similar discussion took place in Sweden, before abortion was legalised. No doctors would be willing to perform abortions at the request of women who did not need to state any reasons for their decision to end their pregnancy, it was maintained. However, when the system was established, doctors did volunteer. The same has happened with respect to euthanasia in the Netherlands. There is no reason to believe that it would not happen in relation to suicide clinics, provided we had good reasons to believe that they could satisfy the requirements discussed here. After all, if we are to have the clinics, in the interest of those who want to commit philosophical suicides, and for the sake of preventing tragic suicides, no other persons than the doctors could do the job at them. The doctors, and no other people, are the experts of how to administer the appropriate drugs in the individual case, in order to guarantee a painless and dignified death of the patient.

This concludes my – inconclusive – discussion of suicide, and the radical proposal of setting up suicide clinics. Let me now return to more mundane problems.

Patients with reduced capacity to reach autonomous decisions

I have indicated that patients suffering from senile dementia or mental impairment (caused by mental retardation, say) pose a special problem in the present context. If these patients need some kind of treatment, but do not agree to undergo it, should society allow doctors or nurses to force the treatment upon them?

It is obvious that, sometimes, in their own best interests, such patients *should* be submitted to coercive care. But it is equally obvious that, in many cases, where these patients *are* being submitted to coercive care, they are being (seriously) wronged. Consequently I raise and try to answer three questions:

1 When should people with these diagnoses be submitted to coercive care?
2 Who should decide about this?
3 Under what legal framework should the medical personnel practising coercive care operate?

If we want to hold on to the principle of respect for the autonomy of the individual in decisions about medical care and social services, there are two temptations that must be resisted. First, we must resist the temptation to paternalistically treat competent people against their will, only because we feel that they do not understand their own best interests. Second, we must resist the temptation to treat competent people against their will because we feel that this is in the best interest of others, such as their relatives, potential victims and health care personnel. Unless we do, people, in general, will not feel safe in their dealings with health care and medical authorities, and unless we do we will not be able to honour a very reasonable ideal of judicial security.

I turn to the first question: when should people who suffer from senile dementia or mental retardation be coercively treated?

Modest vs. meddlesome coercion

Some coercive measures taken towards demented and mentally impaired people in health care situations are warranted, but many such measures are not. As a matter of fact, there exists a long tradition of abuse in relation to these categories of patients. We need a principled answer to the question: which acts of coercion (or manipulation, which I consider an instance of coercion) should be accepted and which should not? I will make use of the terms 'modest' and 'meddlesome' coercion to distinguish between two categories of coercive and manipulative measures, those that are morally acceptable and those that are not.

'Modest' coercion takes place when a patient is forced or manipulated to undergo some medical treatment in a situation where the patient cannot make an autonomous decision in relation to the treatment, rejects the treatment, needs the treatment and is given the treatment in his or her own best interest.

'Meddlesome' coercion takes place when a patient is forced or manipulated to undergo some medical treatment in a situation where the patient *can* make an autonomous decision in relation to the treatment and rejects the treatment. It also takes place when a patient is forced or manipulated to undergo some medical treatment in a situation where the patient cannot make an autonomous decision in relation to the treatment, rejects the treatment and is given the treatment, *not in his or her own best interest, but in the interest of the care-giver*.

The distinction between modest and meddlesome coercion should be sufficiently clear on a conceptual level. However, there are many problems in its application.

Consider the following three patients, all living at one and the same nursing home, but suffering from different degrees of senile dementia. Similar examples can easily be found in the care of mentally impaired persons.

Olga is a 93-year-old woman with no relatives. She is bedridden and weak. She suffers from severe senile dementia and total aphasia. Her peristaltic systems are very inefficient. She needs an aperient desperately. There is a considerable risk that she will develop ileus if she does not take her laxative medicine on a regular basis. However, she refuses her laxative medicine. In spite of the fact that, when fed, she eats with a good appetite, she does not accept *any* medicine. In particular, she shuts her mouth when offered her laxative medicine. The nurse has found a way of giving it to her, all the same. He secretly puts it on a lump of sugar and offers it to Olga, who is fond of sweets. Unbeknownst to herself Olga now takes her medicine. She is successfully manipulated into doing so.

Second, there is Fred, an 85-year-old man, who suffers from senile dementia. He is depressed and he is aggressive. For some time he has been taking anti-depressants. This has made life easier for him and for his care-givers. However, he suddenly refuses to accept the treatment after he has heard that it is given to insane people. He says he is not insane and so he now refuses to accept the medicine. There seems to be no way to convince him. His wife visits him each day and is desperate. She urges the doctor visiting the nursing home to give her husband the medicine, by force if necessary. She wants him to have the medicine for his own sake and for hers. She doubts that her husband fully acknowledges the consequences of his rejection of the medicine. The doctor consults the nurse responsible who agrees to use force. The medicine is given to the man through an injection while several persons hold him.

Third, there is Claire, a 98-year-old woman. She is severely demented and is given diuretic medicine because of her weak heart. Until a month ago, she seemed very satisfied with her life at the home. Then she fractured her hip. She is now bedridden. When food is offered her by a nurse, she refuses to accept it. Her jaw remains shut. Her son, who visits her now and then, claims that she has had enough and does not want to live any more. In particular, he says, there is no point in trying to feed her through a tube against her will. 'Let her go peacefully', he urges the nurse. And so the nurse does. No more food is given to the woman. After a couple of weeks Claire dies.

Were any of the patients subjected to meddlesome coercion? Was the third patient, Claire, abandoned? Was she refused a modest coercion, which should have been given to her, a manipulation that could have saved her life?

Let me start by commenting on the third case. It is not clear from the description of the case whether Claire was correctly treated. Crucial to the assessment is whether she refused to eat because she did not know how to eat – or because she did not want to go on living.

There is no denying that even a patient suffering from severe senile dementia may reach autonomously an answer to the simple, existential question: 'Ought I to go on living?' Even a person who cannot understand the medical effects of various different *medicines* can hold at least an implicit opinion about the *existential* question.

However, it may be very difficult for the nurse to tell what a severely demented person really wants. It takes much compassion, skill and even courage, to ascertain whether Claire's rejection of food expresses her wish to die, or merely her ignorance about eating.

The son's opinion is of some interest but should not determine action. He may not really know his mother, his motives may be mixed, and so forth. I will argue that the responsibility for the decision should rest exclusively with the care-giver.

Consider now the second case, Fred. Here it is tempting to argue that the coercion he was subjected to was modest. When he started to undergo anti-depressant treatment his life quality improved. When he refused to continue the treatment his life quality worsened. To be sure, to have him on the treatment was also in the interest of his care-givers and his wife. However, this does not suffice to show that the coercion was meddlesome. It may still have been given primarily in his own best interests. The satisfaction of the interests of the care-givers and the wife may have been merely a foreseen, positive side-effect of the treatment. The opinion of his wife, that he does not fully acknowledge the consequences of his rejection of the medication, may well be correct.

However, once again we must be careful not to make a rash judgement. First, it might be asked, was the anti-depressant treatment really what he needed? Had all *other* methods of making him comfortable really been tried out?

Suppose, before becoming demented, he loved to play chamber music on an amateur basis. Suppose he had always loved to listen to good recordings of chamber music. Suppose he hates the MTV television programmes, that are offered him at the nursing home. Perhaps it would have sufficed if he had instead been given an opportunity to listen to the music he had always liked.

Second, it might also be asked, was the *way* he was coerced into having the anti-depressant treatment appropriate?

Third, it might be asked whether the man was not after all competent to consider the issue of the drug. A younger person giving the same rationale as Fred for refusing an anti-depressant and in a similar relationship with his wife would most likely be left alone.[11]

It was a quick and easy way out of the problem, but it was also a very brutal one. If the nurse had taken more time with him, there might have been a possibility of reaching some kind of an agreement.

If there is anything to these two considerations, the coercion may well have been very meddlesome indeed.

Let me finally comment on the first case, Olga. This case seems to be the easiest one. If Olga refuses to eat, her decision may well reflect an autonomous decision not to go on living, but Olga eats with good appetite and obviously enjoys her life. However, she does not want to take her medicine and it is not clear why. It is clear, though, that her decision is not an autonomous one. She *cannot* decide autonomously whether she should take it or not. For she does not understand, any more, what an aperient is. And there is no doubt that she needs one. The way she is made to take it is also far less aggressive than Fred's treatment.

When Olga is given her medicine, on a lump of sugar, she is being manipulated to take it, but this manipulation is modest, not meddlesome.

Lessons from the examples

Competency is always relative. A patient may be capable of making an autonomous decision with respect to one problem but not another. This is of crucial importance in the care of mentally impaired persons.

A patient, who is not capable of making an autonomous decision about her aperient may be capable of making an autonomous decision about whether to go on living. In the case of Olga she did want to continue living. Her autonomous decision to go on living deserves our respect. Not to feed her properly would be murder.

---

11 This section of the book draws on my article in *Nursing Ethics* (Tännsjö 1999), and I owe this point to the anonymous reviewer for this journal.

At the same time, a severely demented person's explicit or implicit wish to die, communicated without speech, through a rejection of food is equally worthy of our respect. The patient should not be forced to go on living.

Is it possible to 'err on the right side' here? Is it more problematic not to feed a severely demented old person, who wants to go on living, than to feed a severely demented old person, who wants do die?

I cannot see any moral difference here. To be sure, to make the former kind of mistake is to commit murder. However, to make the latter kind of mistake is very *cruel*; it may indeed come close to torture. So there is no 'safe' way out of the problem. In each case, a decision must be taken, it must be taken one way or the other, both possible mistakes are of equal importance.

This brings us to the question of who should make the decision, in the situation where the patient is not competent to decide. Here we ought to distinguish between two cases, on the one hand the case where a living will exists, and, on the other, the case where no such will exists. I will discuss these cases in order.

Living wills

'Living wills' in this context are understood to be advance directives pertaining to the refusal of medical treatments at the end of life, euthanasia (if permitted), non-resuscitation and abstention from life-sustaining treatment.

Such wills exist in all Western countries but only in some, such as the Netherlands and Denmark, is the use of them regulated in law. In England and Wales there are some examples, where the formal legal validity of such advance statements has been considered: *Airedale Trust* v. *Bland, Re T* and *Re C*.[12] In *Bland* the House of Lords had to decide whether Bland's doctors lawfully could cease his artificial feeding. Bland had been in a persistent vegetative state for three years. In the course of their judgements, Lords Goff and Keith stated that had the patient made an advance decision on the matter, that would have been respected. Thus Lord Keith: 'a person is completely at liberty to decline to undergo treatment, even if the result of his doing so is that he will die. This extends to the situation where the person, in anticipation . . . gives clear instructions. . . .'

Re T concerned an adult pregnant woman injured in a car crash. She refused a blood transfusion which the doctors considered essential to save her life. In the first instance the court allowed the transfusion, on the appli-

---

12 Tor Sverne has drawn my attention to these examples, with the following sources: *Airedale NHS Trust* v. *Bland* (1993) 1 All ER 821; *Re T* (1992) 4 All ER 649; *Re C* (1994) 1 All ER 819.

cation of her father and boyfriend, and the patient *T* appealed. The Appeal Court considered that the doctors were justified in administering blood, first on the ground that *T* was incapable of consenting or refusing because of her medical condition and, second, that her will had been overborne by her mother (who was a Jehovah's Witness). In the course of giving these reasons, Lord Donaldson acknowledged that a doctor could not act 'contrary to a clearly established anticipatory refusal to accept treatment' by the patient.

The final case is that of *Re C* in which a mentally ill patient refused an operation to remove his gangrenous leg. In granting the patient an injunction preventing the hospital from carrying out the operation without his express written consent, Mr Justice Thorpe came to the conclusion that the patient was capable of understanding and retaining the information given to him and in making a decision based on that information. Therefore, despite his mental illness, the patient had the capacity to make an anticipatory refusal of the treatment and the courts had jurisdiction to determine the effect of 'a purported advance directive as to the future medical treatment'.

In the US the aforementioned Patient Self-Determination Act regulates the use of advance directives. Under this law institutions are required to maintain written policies, procedures and records regarding advance directives and institutional obligations under law, and make sure that patients are not discriminated against because they have or have not created an advance directive.

It is obvious that *some* attention should be paid to living wills. This is also guaranteed in the Convention. There it is stated:

> The previously expressed wishes relating to a medical intervention
> by a patient who is not, at the time of the intervention, in a state
> to express his or her wishes shall be taken into account.
>
> (Article 9)

But *how* should such wishes be taken into account? What *weight* should be given to them?

The best system, it seems to me, would be the following. An express living will should be accepted unless there are very special reasons to go against it. In particular no attempts should be made by doctors, nurses or courts to ascertain whether it is really still 'valid', when needed for a decision. After all, 'ordinary' wills are accepted on such terms. The argument from judicial security supports a similar treatment of living wills.

If this is the use we make of living wills, if they are legally binding, it is possible for a person, through a living will, to take precautions that his or her (present) will, rather than the (future) will of doctors or judges, be respected. This is a choice we ought to have, it seems to me.

47

To be sure, we may come to change our mind. Those who believe they will, or those who believe that, in the future, others will know better about their future state of mind than they themselves do now, should not make a living will. However, for those who do not believe this, for those who mistrust the judgement of future doctors or their close relatives, the possibility of writing and registering a legally binding living will should be left open.

By the same token, a register could be kept of people who have strong feelings as to whether their organs should be taken from them, in case they become possible donors of organs for transplantation (if they become 'brain dead').

Of course, no organ should be taken from a person unless this person has previously consented to become a donor, or at least unless it is reasonable to presume that this is what the person actually wanted. This right to an individual veto is necessary in order to safeguard a common trust in the medical system. However, in most cases, in most countries, the procedure where consent is sought is informal. In some countries, such as Austria and Sweden, a presumption exists that people want to donate their organs. Unless they say otherwise (in a written living will, or informally, to their close relatives) it is assumed that they would want to donate their organs.

This is a very practical arrangement. Most people do not want to make formal arrangements. They inform their close relatives about their opinion, and they trust that it will be respected. However, some people may suspect that their will might not be honoured, after all. They may feel that their close relatives may misrepresent their position. Or they may suspect that doctors will manipulate their close relatives into a decision which does not reflect their own will. For these people a living will, which is legally binding, or an official notice in a central register, which cannot be set aside by the doctors, would be a good solution to their problem.

Note that such a living will, or such a register, may be equally important to the person who *wants* his organs to be used to save lives (but fears that close relatives will not allow this), as it would be to the person who *opposes* this (and fears that the doctors will not take his 'no', said to his close relatives, for an answer).

It might be asked whether living wills should also extend to mental illness. In Chapter 5 I will argue that mental illness should be treated in this respect exactly like somatic illness.

Who should decide?

But suppose that no living will exists. In that case, who should decide about the use of coercion in the somatic care for patients suffering from senile dementia or mental retardation?

It is obvious that the responsible doctor or nurse must have a say. Should any *other* party be involved? Should there be a system of 'proxies' making the decision?

In some medical systems the role of a proxy has been institutionalised. This is the case in Spain, for example, where lingering illness or physical or mental retardation (which cause someone with difficulties in taking care of their own interests) can be a reason for a declaration of incapacity. One or more persons can be appointed as guardians. The guardian is responsible for the care and the protection of the incapacitated. Similar systems exist in many countries but in other countries they are absent. This is true of Sweden. Moreover, in one and the same country, the system may vary. This is the case in Canada where the applicable statutory and common law varies across province or territory (Lazar *et al.* 1996).

Some such system is actually required, in the aforementioned Convention on Human Rights and Biomedicine, which is supposed to become binding in the EU, the US, Canada, Japan and Australia, where it is stated:

> Where, according to law, an adult does not have the capacity to consent to an intervention because of a mental disability, a disease or for similar reasons, the intervention may only be carried out with the authorisation of his or her representative or an authority or a person or body provided for by law.

> (Article 3)

I take exception to this system. In my discussion of it I draw from what I consider sound Swedish experience. In Sweden there is no formal role whatever for proxies in these kinds of decisions. And there are good reasons for maintaining such a system.

First of all, as is conceded even by those who share the view of Beauchamp and Childress in their much used textbook, *Principles of Biomedical Ethics*, that it is now 'widely agreed that the patient's closest family member is the first choice as a surrogate' (1994: 244), there is not always such a surrogate person to be found to act as a proxy. Moreover, there may be more than one person claiming this unique status, and it may be impossible to decide who to choose. If the medical personnel take full responsibility for the decision to coerce or not to coerce the patient, then this means that we need not go into the problem of identifying a unique surrogate person at all.

Second, as is also conceded by Beauchamp and Childress (1994: 245), if the proxy is a close relative to the patient, there is no way of ascertaining that the interests of the proxy are not at variance with those of the patient. So for the sake of the security of the patient, no relative should take decisions for the patient. A close relative may be very much concerned about the interests of a patient. However, there is no guarantee of this. The opposite may very well be the case, and there is often no way of telling. For this reason, it is much too hazardous to rely on formal or informal proxies in medical decisions.

It might be objected that when we forgo the possibility of having proxies who are closely related to the patient making medical decisions, we lose competence. For it is an exception rather than the rule that the interests of the proxy run counter to the interests of the patient.

Still, it is better not to rely on proxies but to rely, instead, on the objectivity of the care-giver. For the rare case, where the interests of the proxy conflict with the interests of the patient, may, for all its rarity, be of the utmost importance. It may be a matter of life and death for the patient (and a matter of ruin or prosperity, say, for the proxy).

But could the proxy be a person without personal relations to the patient? I see no point at all in that system. Why not have the care-giver, who knows the patient, who is supposed to be objective and who is supervised by controlling authorities, do the job?

Furthermore, the rejection of a system of proxies need not really mean that the knowledge possessed by close relatives is forgone in medical decisions. When hard choices have to be made, close relatives can and should be consulted by care-givers as *informants*, on behalf of the incompetent patient. Close relatives need not take part in the actual decision in order to convey information to the responsible care-givers.

Third, it is also in the interest of close relatives themselves not to have to take part in hard choices concerning medical measures taken on behalf of an incompetent patient. A decision often has to be made, one way or the other, and there is no way of 'erring on the right side'. As we have seen, *if* mistakes are made in the care of severely mentally impaired people, the mistakes may be very serious. As a matter of fact, they may amount to something close to murder or torture. Furthermore, it is often very difficult to *know* whether a mistake has been committed or not. If people are expected to make decisions on behalf of incompetent relatives, needing medical care, they are encouraged to take a kind of responsibility that may be hard to live with. These people may feel afterwards, correctly or incorrectly, that they made the wrong decision.

Such feelings of guilt may seriously harm them and these feelings may in some rare cases destroy their lives. In any case, such feelings are very difficult to live with. Close relatives should be spared of such feelings. As a member of the ethics committee of the board supervising the Swedish health care system I have come across many such cases.

Is this assessment of mine paternalistic? To some extent it is. However, it represents a modest kind of paternalism which is innocent and hard to avoid within a system of health care. I submit that it is always objectionable when a competent person is being coerced, in his or her own best interests, to adopt one available medical alternative rather than another. However, it is not always objectionable when a competent person is not offered a certain kind of health care choice at all. It is not objectionable, for example, when a patient is not allowed to choose a certain cure against a certain disease, if the reason for not offering the choice is that the choice is considered too *dangerous* for the patient by health care authorities (especially if there are less dangerous alternatives to it).[13] And the kind of paternalism exemplified by medical authorities who refuse to involve relatives in decisions to treat patients coercively is of this latter, innocent kind, rather than of the former, objectionable one. These relatives are not being coerced into any decision in particular.

Should the law distinguish between modest and meddlesome coercion?

We have seen that some coercion of a modest character should be permitted in the care of mentally impaired patients. The decision to take coercive action should be taken by the medical personnel, in most cases by the responsible nurse. However, the coercion and manipulation should not cross the boundary into where it becomes meddlesome. How should this be accomplished? Under what legal framework should the medical personnel operate?

In some countries any coercion considered medically necessary for mentally impaired patients is allowed to the extent that proxies and, in some countries, courts of law, do not block the coercion. This is the case for example in the Netherlands, England and Wales. In other countries no such coercion whatever is permitted. This is the case in Sweden.

It is then tempting to think that the law in *both* these kinds of countries should be revised. Why not try to find a middle way? Why not incorporate a distinction in the law between modest and meddlesome coercion, allowing for the former kind of coercion and prohibiting the latter kind?

I wish I could defend this position. I have made serious efforts to come up with a good defence. However, for reasons to be spelt out below, I have failed. And I have come to think that it is no coincidence that the law is either a masterpiece of hypocrisy, as in Sweden, where modest coercion is prohibited but yet expected to take place, or much too harsh, as in the Netherlands, England and Wales. It is not possible to find a middle way between these two extremes.

The British and Dutch system is not acceptable. It is not desirable that people who can make some kind of decisions concerning their medical

---

13 I discuss this in detail in my article 'The Morality of Clinical Research: A Case Study' (1994).

needs, but not other kinds of decisions, should be deprived of *all* authority over themselves. This is what happens in systems like the British and the Dutch ones.

However, it is also far from ideal that people who need some modest coercive care should only be able to have it if their care-givers dare to break the law. So why not opt for a law that makes the necessary distinction between modest and meddlesome coercion? Well, the main reason is that this is clearly *not possible*. This is to do with the fact, observed above, that one and the same person can be competent in relation to one medical decision but not in relation to another.

To be sure, in an act of law we could have recourse to the notion of decision-specific competency. For example, we could distinguish in the manner that has been indicated by Beauchamp and Childress between different inabilities, such as the inability to express or communicate a preference or choice, to understand one's situation and its consequences, to understand relevant information, to give a reason and so forth (1994: 137). The problem with such a list, however, is that the items on it are *types* of decisions. But when it comes to mentally retarded patients, it is the rule rather than the exception that one and the same patient can be incompetent (at one time) in relation to one token of such a type of decision and competent in relation to another token of the very same type of decision (at another time). Furthermore, the competency of the patient (even in relation to a certain type of decision) tends to decline *gradually*. All this means that, in practice, it is not possible to make all the necessary discriminations in an act of law.

Moreover, if there were a law, then, in the interests of the ideal of judicial security, there should also be procedures to ensure that no one was coerced without the necessary conditions being met. The decision to coerce, in each case, would have to be tried by court of law and so on. We need only contemplate such a system to realise that it would be grotesque.

The choice, then, is between the British and the Dutch system, which is not acceptable, and the Swedish system, which is less than ideal. It seems obvious to me that we should aim, in reforms of the legislative systems in Western countries, towards the Swedish model. After all, it has evolved out of a desire to protect patients from prejudices and abuse.

However, if the decision to use coercion in the care of mentally impaired patients is to be placed in the hands of care-givers who are supposed to exercise coercion in some cases, in spite of the fact that there is a law prohibiting it, where does this leave the ideal of judicial security? Will there be any security for the patients? Will there be any security for the care-givers?

There will be some judicial security for the patients, at least, and this is what is most important. This presupposes, of course, that the use of coercion is always documented. This is imperative. The care-giver should also be obliged to notify the close relatives of the coerced patient. When meddlesome coercion is suspected there is room for complaint. Authorities supervising the care can be addressed. The care-givers, who have documented what they have done, can be held responsible. In the final analysis, the case could be tried before a court of law. If the abuse is serious, the care-givers can be convicted because when coercing the patient, they have violated an act of law.

The case is more difficult when a patient has been abused by having been *denied* modest coercion. Again, a complaint could be filed against the care-givers. In some cases they can be convicted, not of having failed to coerce the patient, which is forbidden, but of not having given the patient appropriate care.

What about the judicial security of the care-givers? Under the suggested kind of laws, their situation is troublesome. It is not nice to regularly have to break the law. However, since this is what is expected from them, it should not be too difficult to do so. Furthermore, even if, in a situation where they have done what they are supposed to and exercised modest coercion, documented what they did, and then a complaint is filed against them, it is to be expected that no actual measures would be taken against them. Even if a prosecutor is brought in, he or she may decide not to bring the case to court.

One could hope for a better system than the one existing for example in Sweden; the Swedish system means that people who are mentally impaired are legally, though not actually, treated as persons who are mentally competent. This is hypocrisy and it is far from ideal. Yet, for all that, the system seems to work to the satisfaction of both patients and care-givers, and since no ideal system is forthcoming, or even possible, hopes for such a system are but vain.

Note also that even if the option taken here has been taken mainly as a default position, there exists one strong argument in defence of it. We all like to think of *ourselves* as competent persons, making autonomous decisions. This may be a mistake, however. If some philosophers who deny that we have a free will turn out to be right, we are not autonomous. Still we want to *think* of ourselves as autonomous. And, more important still, we want to be *treated* as autonomous. If sometimes we were not treated as autonomous beings, we would like to see this as a mere exception to the rule. And it is reasonable to assume that people suffering from senile dementia or mental retardation are no different from us. At least it is clear that they stand to gain if this is taken for granted. In most cases, if we treat them as though they *were* competent, this would mean an increase in the quality of the care they receive.

Conclusion

People suffering from senile dementia or mental retardation should be coercively treated for somatic diseases, in their own best interests, when they need treatment but are incapable of realising this. They should be submitted to what I have called modest coercion. However, these patients should never be submitted to meddlesome coercion, that is, if they understand what kind of treatment they are rejecting, then their 'no' to treatment should be taken for an answer, and they should never be treated in the best interests of others, including the health care personnel, other patients or their relatives.

It would have been neat to have a legal system drawing the line between modest and meddlesome coercion. However, this is not possible to accomplish, since the same patient can be competent in relation to one decision, but not in relation to another decision, at the same time, or competent at one time in relation to one decision, but not competent in relation to the same decision at another time. This means that we have to choose between a law giving too much licence to the health care personnel, or a hypocritical system giving no licence at all, but taking it for granted that they will take (coercive) action when they should, but not otherwise. Drawing on experiences from my own country, Sweden, I have defended the latter hypocritical system.

3

PREVENTIVE HEALTH CARE

The health care system has been designed mainly to cure diseases, when they arise. When no cure is possible, the system has been designed, to an increasing degree, to provide palliative care – and in some cases to shorten life, intentionally or unintentionally, actively or passively (in some rare cases, such as in the Netherlands, *both* intentionally and actively).

Far less systematic effort has been spent on attempts to prevent diseases from arising in the first place. Yet, for all that, we know that preventive measures may be very effective. We know that preventive measures that have been taken primarily for reasons other than to prevent the spread of diseases, such as better hygiene, housing, working conditions and more time for leisure, have been very effective also in improving the health status of the people in modern industrially developed countries. We know also that various vaccination programmes have been very effective in controlling and eradicating diseases. By being careful about what we eat, by the use of regular and moderate exercise and so forth, we can individually enhance our life expectancy.

It is to be expected that preventive health care will be of growing importance in the near future. New methods of preventive medicine develop rapidly. There is a 'market' for them, since there is a gain to be made, of course, if we need not go through a period of illness before we can be cured, but can instead be spared the illness, by taking preventive precautions against it.

Perhaps, if we view the future of medicine in a long-term perspective, we may now be able to anticipate a time when the medical problem has, through preventive measures, been solved: people no longer become ill, they live their full life-span until, satisfied with life, they die because of weakness (or, perhaps more realistically, through physician-assisted suicide). Different forms of handicap are prevented through germline genetic therapy and everyone is born with an effective resistance to all common diseases.

However, this is still in the far future. More mundane problems face us today. Furthermore, there may be diseases that can be prevented but are,

55

as yet, impossible to cure. These diseases pose special problems for preventive medicine.

Just like curative and palliative (somatic) health care, preventive health care measures can give rise to problems relating to coercion. To what extent, if any, may preventive measures legitimately take a coercive form? This is one of the two main problems to be discussed in the present chapter.

As we shall see, in this preventive context, in contradistinction to the curative one, there exists also a strong temptation for political authorities, for putative moral reasons, to *prohibit* the possible use of certain forms of health care measures. Such suggested and existing prohibitions against, for example, certain kinds of medical intervention in assisted procreation, providing the couple with 'the kind of baby they want' (of the 'right' sex or sexual orientation, with the desired physical characteristics and so forth), will also be discussed in the present chapter.

It is indeed a kind of coercion, when people are *stopped* or *hindered* from utilising existing medical techniques, or when doctors are not allowed to provide a kind of medical service they are capable of providing. So it is of the utmost importance to try to learn whether any sound rationale exists for such prohibitions.

As we shall see, the legal situation is very different in different European countries, in the US and in Australia in this respect.

So far I have been speaking rather abstractly about preventive health care measures. Here are some examples of possible preventive health care interventions. Simply by contemplating the list we can understand that many difficult problems must arise if we consider the possibility either of making some of them compulsory, or of prohibiting others:

- measures directed at protection of, or changes in, the environment (in general);
- measures directed at the environment of workplaces;
- vaccination programmes;
- changes in the lifestyle of people in general;
- pre-symptomatic identification of genetically determined risks in individuals;
- pre-symptomatic identification of genetically determined risks in well-defined populations (screening);
- prophylactic therapy against pre-symptomatically identified future diseases or risks for diseases (such as mastectomy because of a certain diagnosed risk for breast cancer);
- pre-natal diagnosis and selective abortion of foetuses with genes for diseases or unwanted characteristics (as a service to individual couples or to populations in the form of screening programmes);

- pre-implantation diagnosis and a choice of fertilised eggs for implantation without disease (or with desired characteristics);
- germline gene therapy, producing children with a 'healthy' genetic constitution.

Systems of criminal justice are sometimes said to have two kinds of preventive functions: individual and general. As we can see from the list above, the same is true of preventive health care measures. These measures can be directed towards an individual (and this is the part of preventive medicine which is of growing importance), or they can be directed towards the public in general (this is the traditional kind of preventive health care). Somewhere in between fall screening programmes.

Here both kinds will be discussed in order and a special note will be made about genetic screening programmes.

Pre-symptomatic diagnosis

In the most spectacular form of pre-symptomatic diagnosis some cells are taken from a person, in a simple, non-invasive fashion, and these cells are submitted to genetic testing. We are only at the beginning of a very rapid development here. The human genome is being identified within the HUGO project, now almost complete. HUGO is a global research project, which was initiated in the late 1980s in the USA, Japan and some European countries. The immediate goal of the project has been DNA sequencing as well as identifying and mapping the place of every gene within its appropriate chromosome. Another goal has been to understand how genes act and interact in human development and in aetiologies of human pathology. This understanding is expected to provide the impetus for major advances in the future of health care, the development of medical science and public health policy.

It is expected that the application of new genetic knowledge obtained through this project will allow the possibility of the prevention, diagnosis and treatment, not only of inherited monogenetic diseases, such as phenylketonuria, cystic fibrosis, thalassaemia, etc., but of a wide spectrum of other diseases as well. These include cardiovascular diseases, diabetes, some forms of cancer, mental and neurological disorders, infectious diseases (including TB and AIDS), all of which are widespread and involve (complex) genetic and environmental factors. An even more spectacular possibility is that genes for physical characteristics and personality traits will be identified.

Further, if it is possible to diagnose the predisposition before the appearance of the disease (pre-symptomatic diagnosis), it might be possible to implement preventive measures such as changes in lifestyle and periodic check-ups, or to administer gene therapy in the future.

There is no need to go any further into medical detail here, nor to specify any detailed future scenario. For the kind of discussion to be pursued it is enough to note that, undoubtedly, for *many* (important) diseases, and for *some* physical characteristics and personality traits, it will be possible to find a genetic cause.

Where does this leave the health care system? Should the health care system provide *any* kind of service that is in its power to deliver? Should some kind of testing be compulsory (for example, when insurance is bought or when a job is sought)?

From what has been said so far in this book it should be clear that, in my opinion, a strong presumption exists in defence of a system where *any* service that *can* be delivered, *should* be delivered, on request.

To be sure, some provisos must be met here. The service should be of a respectable medical and scientific standard. And, to the extent that it is publicly financed, it should compete successfully with other services in a consideration of where the strongest medical priorities are. However, if delivered outside the public system, costs are not important. No one should be stopped from spending all his or her economic resources on a preventive measure, just because it is not considered to be in his or her best interests. The individual is the best judge of his or her own medical needs.

This runs counter to medical practice in many countries. All sorts of provisos are being constructed and upheld. It has been said, for example, that unless there exists a cure, or some other preventive measures that can be taken, no diagnosis should be offered for a genetic disease. And it has been said that, unless the disease is serious, no diagnosis should be offered. There is no good rationale for this sort of social meddling with the decisions of the individual.

Take the case of diseases for which there is no cure. One much discussed example is Huntington's corea. If a person who knows that the odds that he carries the gene for the disease are 50/50 (i.e. one of his parents had the disease) does not want to know whether the probability is actually 1 or 0, he should have the right *not* to obtain this information. If, on the other hand, he wants to know, he has a right to know, or so I am prepared to argue.

The desire to know may be rational. After all, this person may want to plan his life. If, as a matter of fact, he knows that he will develop the disease, he may opt for one lifestyle (to pursue his career and have no family, for example), or, if he knows he will not, he may opt for a different lifestyle (if possible, with a family).

What about diseases less awful than Huntington's corea, then? What about genes for mere physical and personality *characteristics*?

It seems to be part of received opinion that the individual should be prohibited from seeking such information. This is also prohibited in the Convention, which states:

Tests which are predictive of genetic diseases or which serve either to identify the subject as a carrier of a gene responsible for a disease or to detect a genetic predisposition or susceptibility to a disease may be performed only for health purposes or for scientific research linked to health purposes, and subject to appropriate genetic counselling.

(Article 12)

Again, it is not difficult, however, to conceive of situations where such information, with no relation to any health purposes as such, or any scientific research linked to health purposes, may be of the utmost importance to the individual.

Consider an 18-year-old woman, who contemplates whether she should continue or give up her efforts to become a top athlete. There seems to be some way still to go for her, before she reaches her peak, and perhaps the goal is not quite unrealistic. She takes a genetic test of a kind that may be feasible in the future, finds out that her genetic odds are poor (she may become a very good athlete, but not among the very best ones), and opts instead for another career.

Or, consider a person who wants to become a politician, but is not certain that he will not develop into a ruthless and positively dangerous person, if he does. He takes a genetic test, of a future possible kind, and finds out that, unless he takes precautions, he may very well come to develop a psychopathic personality (doing, in the political context, much harm); he takes this news seriously, we assume, and opts instead for his second-best alternative: he becomes a painter and a loner (minimising the probability that he will become a psychopath as well as the harm he will be able to do, if, after all, he does become one).

Or, to give one more example, consider a young man who is uncertain as to his sexual orientation. Suppose that there are genes for sexual orientation and suppose that these can be identified. We do not at present know whether there are genes for sexual orientation (I will return to this question below when discussing pre-natal diagnosis), but *suppose* there are. Would it not be a good thing to know one's sexual orientation, even if this has nothing to do with health care or science? In particular, would it not be easier to 'come out' as a homosexual, if one knew that one had an inborn bent for homosexuality? Would not this also render easier the explanation to one's parents of one's sexual preferences?

If no one should be prohibited from undergoing whatever pre-symptomatic tests he or she sees fit, the question remains whether such tests should ever be compulsory.

Here our moral intuitions revolt strongly against the idea that they should be, I think, and they do so correctly. These intuitions probably explain why some people want to *forbid* some kind of pre-symptomatic testing. The people with these strong intuitions may believe that, if people are allowed to undergo such testing, there is a definite risk that what is permissible today will become obligatory tomorrow.

This fear is real, but it should be possible to control such temptation. The temptation arises mainly in two situations, when people want to buy life insurance and when people apply for jobs with certain requirements. It might be tempting for insurance companies and for employers to require genetic tests from those who want to buy life insurance or apply for a job.

Both these possible applications of genetic testing are ruled out by Article 12 of the Convention, quoted above, and they should be forbidden, it seems to me. They have also been ruled out, earlier, by the Council of Europe in Recommendation No. R (90) 13.

The job case is most easily dealt with. Since most people feel that it is of importance to them that their genetic integrity be protected, society can simply forbid employers to seek genetic information from their employees, or from persons who seek employment. When such information was not available, there was no real problem for employers in doing without it. So it should be possible for employers to do without it today and in the future as well, provided that *no* employer is allowed to gain access to it. In a competitive structure, it is crucial, of course, that the same rules apply to all. It is less important, however, what these rules are!

The insurance case is more complicated. If people are allowed to gain privileged access to information about their genetic status, and then buy life insurance as they see fit, there is a possibility that some, who find that they have genes for a disease that will seriously shorten their lives, will buy very expensive life insurance and thus exploit other buyers of the insurance. If this phenomenon becomes extensive, there is a real danger that the insurance system will suffer or break down.

I consider this a real threat to a *private* insurance system. However, this is no reason to *forbid* individuals from seeking genetic advice, nor is it a reason *not* to forbid insurance companies from seeking the same advice – at least, not if a *public* health care system exists, providing all the care and security needed for people in any kind of physical or mental distress.

This may seem to be a strong political assumption on which to rest the case for freedom (in order to have individual freedom to seek genetic advice and respect for genetic privacy we must have a public health care system); however, here the scientific development *as such* seems to conspire against a too libertarian politics.

After all, the commercial insurance system is built on the idea that there is ignorance about the future. The more predictable our medical future is, the less suitable is an insurance system to redistribute resources between people and over the life cycle of the individual. When we know our future, we *need* some kind of tax system to achieve the necessary redistribution.

So if future developments of techniques for pre-symptomatic testing may prove devastating to systems of private health insurance, life insurance and medical insurance, this is as it should be; it is only to be expected and it should be accepted. When private insurance becomes impossible, the public health care system should take over responsibility for the individual, even in countries that are to this date dominated by private health care provisions.

Selective abortion, pre-implantation diagnosis and germline gene therapy

Not only can a genetic diagnosis be obtained for an existing individual. The same can also be achieved for foetuses during pregnancy, for pre-embryos (fertilised eggs, zygotes, blastulae and so forth) and gametes, before implantation. Again a presumption for free choice exists. Who is supposed to know better than the prospective parents (or simply, the prospective mother) what kind of preventive health care measures should be taken? The parents know what kind of disease of, or characteristics in, the future child they are prepared to take responsibility for.

However, in this field, it is part of received opinion, and indeed of the laws in European states, that some restrictions must be made.

Some countries are very strict, such as Germany, Norway and Sweden, where not even in combination with in vitro fertilisation (IVF) is the dona-tion of eggs or semen allowed, let alone the donation of embryos or the lending of one's uterus (surrogate motherhood). In many countries, no laws at all regulate the use of IVF (this used to be the case in Denmark and is still the case in Finland). In the UK and in France there are laws regulating the use of IVF, legalising donation of egg and semen.[1] The differences between different countries may sometimes seem strange. In Norway storage of oocytes is prohibited while storage of embryos is allowed. In Germany storage of oocytes is allowed while storage of embryos is prohibited. This means that, while eggs *undergoing* fertilisation are classified in Norway as early embryos they are classified as eggs in Germany! All Western countries allow (legally or informally) for some kind of pre-natal diagnosis, rendering possible selective abortion of foetuses with serious diseases, but in many countries there exist informal restrictions of the right to pre-natal diagnosis. And no country allows that germline gene therapy takes place (would it become a possibility).

Does a sound rationale exist for the opinion that some restrictions are in order in this field? *Should* any such restrictions be made?

---

1 I have these facts from a report from the Swedish Council for Medical Ethics (1995-04-19) on assisted reproduction and from the recent report, *Reproductive Medicine and Embryo-logical Research: A European Handbook on Bioethical Legislation* (MacKellar, 1997).

Two questions come to mind. First, should there be kinds of diagnosis or intervention that the individual should be *prohibited* from seeking? Second, should there be kinds of intervention that it be *obligatory* for the individual to undergo?

Let me start with the former question: are there any feasible kinds of intervention, that should be forbidden? Does a sound rationale exist for any of the existing prohibitions in some European countries?

Germline gene therapy

I think there is no such rationale. This is a radical claim. How could it be defended?

A sound strategy in defence of my radical liberal claim would be to focus on those applications that strike some as most abhorrent. What comes to mind most naturally, then, is germline gene therapy. In germline gene therapy the genome of gametes or a pre-embryo is changed, with the result that the new, altered or added genes, can be inherited by future children of the manipulated individual.

If anything should be restricted, it is germline genetic therapy, it may seem. On the other hand, should germline genetic therapy be something that prospective parents could seek, to the extent they see fit, then all sorts of intervention should be allowed, or so most people would be prepared to say, with, perhaps one proviso: the selection of sex or sexual orientation (through selective abortion or pre-implantation diagnosis) should not in general be allowed, some would argue.

In the Convention germline gene therapy is strictly forbidden:

> An intervention seeking to modify the human genome may only be undertaken for preventive, diagnostic or therapeutic purposes and only if its aim is not to introduce any modification in the genome of any descendants.
>
> (Article 13)

And in Article 14, sex selection is prohibited while the selection of sexual orientation is not mentioned:

> The use of techniques of medically assisted procreation shall not be allowed for the purpose of choosing a future child's sex, except where serious hereditary sex-related disease is to be avoided.

I discuss germline gene therapy in this section, taking it for granted that, if germline gene therapy can be allowed on request, then so can pre-implantation diagnosis, as well as pre-natal diagnosis. I return to the question of the selection of sex or sexual orientation in the next section.

I cannot go into detail here. In particular, I will say nothing about what I consider poor arguments against germline gene therapy. A reason for being brief is that I have discussed the problem in more detail elsewhere (Tännsjö 1993), as have others such as Jonathan Glover (1984, 1989), Ruth Macklin (1977) and John Harris (1993). In the present context, let me just adumbrate my argument.

The reason for *allowing* germline gene therapy is straightforward. If it became possible to safeguard one's children from certain diseases through germline gene therapy, this would be a very natural choice. If a genetic 'vaccination' could be developed against, for example, some not unusual diseases, such as cancer, coronary heart disease, AIDS or Alzheimer's, if the procedure was safe, and if it was best administered to the fertilised egg (in combination with in vitro fertilisation), then to give this vaccination to one's prospective child would be a good idea.

I would not hesitate to give it to *my* children. After all, if I did forgo this possibility, and my children came to suffer from any one of these diseases, how should I, when they asked me, defend my decision of not having 'vaccinated' them?

This is perhaps not very controversial. I suppose that what is controversial is that other kinds of uses of the method should also be allowed. Or, what is controversial is that even these rational uses of the method should be allowed, considering that there is a risk that other, less rational uses, might also be made of it. Would not this mean that some parents, who suffered from lack of self-respect, or self-esteem, would try to impose various different compensatory ideals upon their children, it could be asked.

I suppose that this fear is the rationale behind the strong prohibition of germline gene therapy stated in the Convention. Since no such therapy is possible for the moment, it is also very easy to reach the decision that it should be forbidden. My conjecture is, however, that once it becomes possible to prevent serious diseases through germline genetic intervention, such intervention will, as a matter of fact, take place. However, what about the risks that such a system would deteriorate?

The following scenario could be sketched. Those who failed as athletes might like to make perfect athletes out of their children, those who failed as musicians might like to give their children perfect pitch, those who failed as mathematicians might like to seek mathematical skill for their children. And would not this mean a kind of terror for their children?

I suppose it would. And it should not give us pause that some of the applications discussed above may prove impossible. For, to be sure, others not discussed here may instead prove possible. There is no guarantee whatever that no applications of this kind will be possible. So the question is real.

However, it should be noted that what these children would suffer from are not really the characteristics that are sought for them by their parents.

Accidentally, they could have received these very same characteristics anyway. Other children do receive them, without being subjected to germline gene therapy. They do not suffer because of this. What these children, with parents acting out of compensatory needs, do suffer from are, rather, these compensatory needs, which have such a grip on their parents, with or without possible access to gene therapy; these children are not really suffering from the therapeutic measures as such, taken pre-natally, or at the pre-implantation stage, but from the ambitions of their parents.

Something should be done, if possible, to correct such parents' compensatory needs, of course, but this is not a problem that is best dealt with through compulsory social measures. Education of some kind seems rather to be what should be prescribed for these parents.

However, would not germline gene therapy be dangerous? Would it not be so dangerous that it should not be contemplated?

Of course it could be dangerous, but this is not a principled argument against it. Standard precautions must be taken, if it is ever allowed. But there is no reason to believe that it must be *so* dangerous, that it should *never* be contemplated.

After all, some important gains may come to be made through this kind of medical technique. And the hazards involved in its use may prove to be of an 'ordinary' nature.

The selection of sex or sexual orientation

Ought it not at least be forbidden for parents to choose children of a certain sex, or a certain sexual orientation? More generally, ought not society allow prospective parents, through selective abortion, pre-implantation diagnosis and genetic therapy, to avoid certain handicaps and diseases, but not, positively, to choose to have babies with certain characteristics, where sex and sexual orientation are just two among all those possible? As we saw above, this is in line with the stance taken up in the Convention.

At first this stance may seem compelling. However, how would a good argument in defence of it go? I suppose that medical and political authorities would have to argue roughly in the following manner. I concentrate first on the question of sex.

If people are allowed to choose children of a certain sex, then there is a danger that the sex ratio would be upset, which is an evil (note that this is a concern for the status of the gene pool, i.e. it is a kind of 'eugenic' consideration that will be discussed below in relation to the Nazi experience). And even if the effects on the sex ratio were negligible, the very possibility of avoiding a child of a certain sex would be a signal that the sex commonly selected against was inferior to the sex commonly selected for. Again, this is an evil.

Now, in many countries, in particular in many Western countries, we do not know that any sex in particular would be selected for. Perhaps parents would like to have children of both sexes. They seek a perfect 'mix' in their reproductive decisions. I see no harm in this.

But even if, in a certain country, we know that one sex will be systematically selected against, there is a positive danger in allowing society to meddle with the reproductive decisions of the individual. If medical and political authorities rule that it is permissible to select against certain handicaps, such as, for example, Down's syndrome, but not against any sex in particular, and if the reason given is that one sex is no less valuable than the other, the message given is that *Down's syndrome* does bring with it a life which is less valuable than a more 'ordinary' life. Now, if this is the case, people living with Down's syndrome may come to feel that they are not welcome. They may even come to feel a threat to their very existence![2]

So, upon closer examination, it is a much better policy for society not to form any ideals at all in this area, allowing prospective parents to make whatever reproductive decisions they see fit. A change in the sex ratio may well be, in many respects, something evil, but it is a kind of evil a society may have to live with, for some time.

However, if one sex is systematically selected against, then this fact may reflect widespread prejudice against this sex. If these prejudices can be expressed in decisions to do with reproductive medicine, does this not mean that they gain in momentum? Not necessarily, it seems to me. After all, the problem here is not the medical techniques as such but rather the prejudices.

In most societies where one sex in particular (the female sex) is systematically being selected against using new techniques (in India, for example), the same sex has previously been selected against as well, only through other, more mundane (and more cruel) techniques, such as the spending of less medical effort on girls, and giving them less food than boys, and even, in some cases, the active killing of the girls.

There should exist more effective ways of counteracting these prejudices than by society prohibiting prospective parents (in particular women) from using advanced reproductive techniques.

Once again, what comes to mind is education, laws against sex discrimination and so forth, rather than coercive intervention in the reproductive decisions taken by prospective parents.

2 This and similar fears have been voiced over and over by representatives of the handicap movement in Sweden. For an excellent review of the discussions in Sweden about pre-natal diagnosis and pre-implantation diagnosis, see Christian Munthe's two books, *The Moral Roots of Prenatal Diagnosis: Ethical Aspects of the Early Introduction and Presentation of Prenatal Diagnosis in Sweden* (1996) and, *Pure Selection: The Ethics of Pre-implantation Genetic Diagnosis* (forthcoming).

My argument concerning the selection of sexual orientation is similar. We do not know to what extent this will be possible. But to the extent that sexual orientation is genetically determined,[3] selection procedures are likely to become available. Now, if the selection of sexual orientation becomes possible, and we forbid it while allowing selection against, say, mental retardation, society gives the message that, while there is nothing wrong with being gay, there is something wrong with being mentally retarded. This is not acceptable. Those who are mentally retarded are even more in need of protection against prejudice than are homosexuals. After all, in most societies, prejudices against mentally retarded people are deeper and more widespread than prejudices against homosexuals.

If selection of sexual orientation becomes possible and is allowed, and if people are allowed to make a choice *for* whatever orientation they see fit, then society is indeed neutral. I suppose that most people will not bother to use these techniques. However, even if some do, and even if it turns out that heterosexuals select for heterosexual children while homosexuals select for homosexual children, this need not affect the ratio in society between heterosexuals and homosexuals. It may mean that the gulf between the two cultures deepens, however, and this may mean problems for children who happen to be born in the 'wrong' culture. This is likely to happen now and then, since foolproof selection procedures will never exist.

On the other hand, the fact that those who have *strong* prejudices against the 'other' sexual orientation will rarely have children of the 'undesired' orientation, may prove to be a good thing for their children. Still, these prejudices pose a social problem.

How should society deal with this problem? Well, once again I suppose that the proper way to deal with the problem is through education, laws against discrimination on the grounds of sexual orientation and so forth, rather than coercive intervention in the reproductive decisions taken by prospective parents.[4]

Should society force parents to use preventive health care medicine in their peproductive decisions?

Let me now turn to a discussion of the question of whether parents should sometimes be compelled to undergo preventive treatment, because of a concern for the health of the future child.

3 See Dean Hamer *et al.* 'A Linkage between DNA Markers on the X Chromosome and Male Sexual Orientation' (1993) for putative evidence for the fact that male sexual orientation has a genetic basis. But see also William Byne, 'The Biological Evidence Challenged' (1994), for a critique.
4 For an argument to the opposite effect, i.e. to the effect that the selection of sexual orientation is special and should be forbidden, see Edward Stein, 'Choosing the Sexual Orientation of Children' (1998).

In this context the anti-paternalist argument breaks down. If we coerce the parents, we coerce them not in their own best interests, but in the best interests of the future child. This is not paternalism.

Here also the argument from judicial security breaks down, at least in its most general application. I will argue in chapters to come that, for reasons to do with judicial security, society should never use medical measures as punishment. However, if we coerce prospective parents in the interests of their prospective children, we coerce them, not as a way of punishing them, but as a way of stopping them from actually bringing misfortune upon their prospective children. It is at least not obvious that this must be at variance with the ideal of judicial security.

As a matter of fact, a strong presumption exists for coercing prospective parents to take preventive health care measures for the sake of their future children. A strong presumption exists even for society to try to ascertain whether a person should be allowed to have children in the first place. A presumption exists for only allowing good and capable persons to have children, and for only allowing them, to the extent that this can be controlled, to have children who are capable of living a life worth living. After all, what could be more important than that each individual who is born is born to a life worth living, and that each individual who is born has parents capable of providing a loving and caring upbringing of it?

So when I want to argue *against* this presumption, a strong and extra-ordinary argument is needed. The argument I want to rely on has to do with the Nazi experience. Three important features characterised the Nazi practice.

First, the Nazis were prepared to *prescribe* how a life should be shaped in order to be a *worthy* life. A life below the threshold, *as defined by medical and political authorities*, was a '*lebensunwertig Leben*' and should, in the early Nazi practice, be prevented from beginning (through compulsory sterilisation) and, later on in the Nazi practice, be killed (a kind of murder that the Nazis misnamed 'euthanasia').

Second, the Nazis defined what it meant for a life to be a worthy life, not out of concern for the individual living the life in question, but, rather, out of concern for the race (the gene pool, to use up-to-date terminology). Their concern was not with how the life was experienced, 'from the inside', by the person living it, their concern was not with whether, from this person's own perspective, it was worth living, but with its contribution to more abstract ideals. Their concern was that the race (the gene pool) be in good shape.

Finally, the Nazis were prepared to use, not only coercion, but violence (including murder), to implement their medically and politically defined ideals.

The Nazis proved that the use of medicine for political means can be very dangerous. There is no denying that new medical inventions, such as new genetic technologies in general, and germline gene therapy in particular, could be misused in a similar manner. It is fair to say that a Nazi Spectre exists. How, then, are we to avoid the Nazi spectre from manifesting itself?

We have to act contrary to the Nazis on all three aspects discussed above, it seems to me.

First, we should see to it that medical and political authorities do not form any ideal whatever about a worthy life. The forming of such an ideal is not an objective for medical or political authorities at all. Reproductive decisions should be made by prospective parents and by no one else.

Second, as individuals, making reproductive decisions, we have a moral obligation to look to the best interests of our prospective children. We should try to look at their possible future life from *their* point of view, so far as we can.

There is no denying that a life may prove not worth living. However, when this is the case, it is the case because such a life is dominated by suffering, frustration and impaired capacities for the child, not because the child would not be a good 'investment' from the point of view of racial interests (from the point of view of considerations to do with the status of the gene pool). Neither the political authorities nor the individual couples need concern themselves with the status of the gene pool.

Finally, since medical and political authorities are not to have opinions in the field, there is simply no room for social coercive interference in our reproductive decisions.

All this may seem quite acceptable as a general policy, but are there no exceptions from it, it might be asked? In particular, should not society, in the interests of the prospective child, stop parents from having severely handicapped children, if this is something that can, through the use of genetic diagnosis, selective abortion, pre-implantation diagnosis or gene therapy, be avoided?

We should resist this argument. Note, first of all, that, even diseases and handicaps like Huntington's corea and Down's syndrome are compatible with a good life. To be sure, it could be argued that it is better that children without these handicaps and diseases are born, rather than children with them. However, even if this is true it may *also* be true that a child *with* such a handicap or disease may consider it a good thing that it was born. Such a child may well live a life worth living. So, all things being equal, there is a case for saying that a world with this child is a better world than a world without it.[5]

This is not to say that there are no hereditary diseases that are so grim that a life with them is worse than no life at all. There are indeed such

5 In 'Who Are the Beneficiaries?' (1992) I give reasons for this thesis of mine.

hereditary diseases. However, these diseases are very rare (there is a considerable number of such diseases, but very few people are affected by any of them). Furthermore, it is not likely that prospective parents, who are provided with medical assistance, will opt for having these children, anyway. So there is very little need for compulsory action in the field.

I think therefore that it is better not to make *any* exceptions from the rule that society should not coercively meddle with the reproductive decisions of the individual. The danger of misuse is very real as soon as we leave *any* room for coercion in the field.

For example, we ought to allow that those who want to do so opt for not having, say, deaf children. This is not to discriminate against deaf people, for, by the same token, militant deaf parents will have a possibility of selecting against hearing children. Not that I believe that this would ever happen, but the mere possibility of it is a guarantee that society is neutral in the field. Society does not meddle with the reproductive choices of citizens.

Even if the *intention* behind coercive measures taken by political authorities over reproductive choices of citizens may be of the very best, such as, for example, to prevent sexual discrimination or the birth of 'wrongful lives', there is a danger in allowing this kind of intervention. If it goes wrong, it may go seriously wrong.

And since the possible gains with such intervention are dubious, we may safely place the decision in the hands of prospective parents, even in cases where this may, at first, seem controversial.

Prospective parents will now and then make foolish and even immoral reproductive decisions, but so would political authorities, were they allowed to regulate procreation. And in general, when individuals make mistakes, the consequences are less serious than when political authorities make them. When political authorities err in this field, the consequences may well prove devastating.

Should anyone be allowed to become a parent?

A question I have touched upon in the foregoing argument is whether anyone who wants to become a parent should be allowed to become one. Should not at least people who are obviously not fit to raise children be forbidden to do so?

If the answer to this question is in the affirmative, a nasty further question emerges: what form should such sanctions take? I suppose the only possible measure would be compulsory sterilisation.

Since this is indeed a very nasty idea, and an idea strongly reminiscent of the Nazi experience (even if compulsory sterilisation took place in many other countries, such as the US, England and Sweden, especially during the 1930s),[6] it is consoling to realise that there exists no good argument in defence of it, or so I will argue, at any rate.

It might be tempting to argue that there are examples of people who, for simple medical reasons, are not fit to raise children. For example, it might be impossible for severely handicapped people to take care of their children. However, if these prospective parents live in a civilised society, all sorts of measures should be taken to help these people to live as 'normal' a life as is possible. And part of a normal life for a couple who can have children, and who want to have children, is to have children. Society should assist them both in reproducing (offer them IVF, if this is what they need) and in taking care of their children.

Now, if a certain prognosis could be made, and if it could be ascertained that a certain couple, or a certain individual, could not become good parents (a good parent), then there would at least be a case for social interference. However, it is obvious that no such prognosis can be made.

To be sure, some variables may make it unlikely that a prospective parent will be able to see to the best interests of a prospective child. And, to the extent that these variables are medical, we can improve our capacity for predicting them. However, these variables are not only medical, but social as well; and, typically, they are not of causal but merely statistical significance. And if we do not want to rule out prospective parents on social (and merely probabilistic) grounds, then, for reasons to do with the ideal of judicial security (the requirement of consequentiality), we should not rule them out on medical grounds either.

Where does this leave the child when the parents fail? Society must intervene, in the best interests of the child, of course. Society should offer help and support to the parent. If the attempts to provide the child with a good upbringing fail, society should take custody of the child from the parents.

Should anyone who needs assisted procreation of any sort really be provided with all available reproductive techniques? Should a person with cystic fibrosis be provided with IVF? And, if he is, should he also have the right to use pre-implantation diagnosis to ensure that he does not pass on the gene for the disease to his children? Should a single homosexual woman have the right to donor insemination?

The ideal of judicial security speaks strongly in favour of such liberal practices. Once again, how could it be possible, prospectively, to select those who are fit to rear children? Must not a selective procedure come to flout the ideal of judicial security?

---

6 I have myself discussed the recent argumentation about the Swedish sterilisation laws in 'Compulsory Sterilisation in Sweden' (1998), where I defend the point made even in the present context: society should not regulate who are allowed to become parents. For a discussion of the US experience, see Philip R. Reilly, 'Eugenic Sterilization in the United States' (1985).

However, when people are allowed licence to use techniques of assisted procreation, even techniques where, in the process, the notions of fatherhood and motherhood become muddled (such as when a surrogate mother lends her uterus to a couple, or when a donor of gametes intervenes in the procreative process and makes it possible for a single homosexual woman to have a child), society should regulate the situation legally, with the best interests of the child as its focus of attention. The point of departure should be family law, not contract law, it seems to me. A good argument to that effect has been given by A.M. Capron and M.J. Radin (1988). In particular, the law should see to it that, for *each* child, *some* person is responsible for it, *qua* social parent, and that, at most, *one* person is considered the social *mother* of the child and, at most, *one* person is considered the social *father* of the child.

A general right to procreate should be safeguarded, then, by society, but not a general right to 'one's' children. As was remarked in the previous chapter, people do not *own* their children.

Genetic screening

Genetic screening, i.e. genetic diagnosis provided for a well-defined population, invited to take a certain test, is sometimes distinguished from genetic diagnosis, given on an individual basis. In a genetic screening programme, society makes an active endeavour to test a population. However, even a screening programme may be voluntary. It is here assumed that it is.

A screening programme can be directed towards providing pre-symptomatic testing but it can also be directed towards providing pre-natal diagnosis. The question now arises: are there any special moral problems in relation to screening programmes?

It might seem that there are none, insofar as the testing is voluntary. So, if people should be free to seek whatever genetic advice they see fit in individual cases, could not society offer whatever kind of diagnosis *it* sees fit to certain well-defined populations?

There is a crucial difference, however, between genetic diagnosis undertaken on an individual basis, and a screening programme, where society *encourages* people (a certain well-defined population) to join in the programme. While the Convention, as well as an earlier recommendation from the Council of Europe (No. R (90) 13), are too restrictive in individual cases, allowing only that tests be made on strictly medical indications, they are too lenient when it comes to screening programmes, allowing for all sorts of investigations, it seems to me.

When society allows the individual to take whatever measures the individual sees fit, society adopts a neutral stance towards various possible results of a genetic diagnosis. The situation is different, in particular in relation to pre-natal diagnosis, when society initiates a screening programme.

Suppose that it was decided to initiate a screening programme offering a test to pregnant women over a certain age as to whether their foetuses will be born with Down's syndrome (which seems to be in conformity with Recommendation No. R (90) 13 on pre-natal genetic screening, pre-natal genetic diagnosis and associated genetic counselling, issued by the Council of Europe). Would this not send the message to pregnant women that they ought to undergo the test and, if the test is positive, have an abortion?

I think it would. And, if such a programme was initiated, publicised and so forth, it would not be far-fetched to imagine that people *with* Down's syndrome would become somewhat uneasy.

For this reason, I think *no* pre-natal genetic screening programmes ought to take place. All sorts of services, that are scientifically feasible and safe, should be offered to the public (the individual pregnant woman should be allowed to seek all sorts of information about her foetus), but no special effort should be invested by society in having people (well-defined populations) make use of any one of them in particular.

The situation may be different with pre-symptomatic testing. A group at risk may be identified and offered a (voluntary) test, preceded by, and followed up by, counselling. However, this seems a reasonable choice for society to make only if there is some cure, or at least some kind of medical advice, that can be offered to these people.

To change people's lifestyle

I now turn to general (rather than individual) preventive health care measures taken by society. There are numerous such measures and many among them involve coercion. I think of such things as the legal provision that those who ride cars use safety belts, that those who ride motorbikes wear a helmet, regulation of the use of drugs and so forth.

Are not these regulations clearly at variance with the principle of respect for personal autonomy that I have stated? Furthermore, are not these regulations very reasonable? So, does not this show that there is something wrong with the principle of respect for personal autonomy?

It is true that these regulations pose a problem for the principle I want to defend. However, the problem is less serious than might at first appear.

Note that the principle should not be interpreted as forbidding that people should be guarded against their own individual irrationality by political means. And this is one possible interpretation of the laws forbidding us to drive or ride motorcycles without safety belts or helmets. They can be seen as political safeguards against our own individual irrationality, freely adopted by us.

To be sure, political theorists and representatives of the dismal science very often make the very opposite point. They are used to saying that, while fully rational and prudent in personal affairs, people become irrational and childish, when it comes to political decisions. Joseph Schumpeter, for example, has famously argued that:

> the typical citizen drops down to a lower level of mental performance as soon as he enters the political field. He argues and analyses in a way which he would readily recognize as infantile within the sphere of his real interests. He becomes a primitive again. His thinking becomes associative and affective.
>
> (1943: 166)

However this may be in general, interestingly enough, there are exceptions from this rule. There *are* cases where, individually, we are obviously *irrational* while, *qua* political agents, we are *rational*.

For many persons, the regulations regarding the use of safety belts and helmets provide good illustrations of this. We know that, if we are allowed not to take these precautions, we will forgo them. However, when sitting down in a reflective moment, we do not want to forgo them. We see the point in using safety belts and helmets. We are prepared to vote for an act of law making their use obligatory. We *want* to be coerced into using them; and this is why we are, in many European countries, in North America and in Australia, coerced into using them.

However, some people may not accept this argument. They may actually want to put their lives at (an extra) risk when riding cars or motorcycles. They resent the laws making the use of safety belts and helmets obligatory. How are we to respond to them, if they complain that these laws express an illegitimate paternalism?

We could try the following answer. We could argue that the reason that they should wear safety belts and helmets is not that this is in their own best interests, but that it is in the best interests of society. If they don't use safety belts and helmets, there is an increased risk that they will be hurt and that all of us, in our role as taxpayers, will have to pay for their lack of risk aversion. After all, we all pay, to a considerable degree, for health care services that are provided for people who get hurt in traffic accidents; at least this is true in most European countries.

This answer may satisfy some of the critics. However there may remain some who do not accept this answer. They may argue that, if necessary, they are prepared to pay for the right to ride their car or motorcycle, without using any safety belt or helmet. What are we to say to these people?

Well, *if* there are such people, and *if* the preventive measures taken by society are of great concern to them, I think these people should come forward and voice their concern. If they do, we should grant them their right. These people should be allowed to pay for the extra burden they cause the taxpayers, by being offered a special health care insurance. If they buy the insurance, they should be allowed to drive their car or ride their motorcycle, without using either safety belt or helmet. In their driver's licence, a note could be made about this special right of theirs.

Vaccination programmes

No one should be forced to undergo vaccination only in his or her own best interests. However, sometimes it might be of crucial importance to the effectiveness of a vaccination programme that enough people join it. Does this mean that there is room here for legitimate coercion?

I think it does. However, there is rarely any need for such coercive measures. In most cases, enough people join the programme voluntarily. The problem may rather be the opposite one, and therefore economical. The problem is often that more people than are necessary to ascertain medical success want to join the programme. If they are allowed to do so, this means a waste of resources. However, it is hard to deny *some* people this possibility. This could be achieved through a lottery. However, in the present context, the idea of a lottery is not likely to win support.

A solution to this problem might be to render the procedure where informed consent is sought, and obtained, quite complicated. It could be made precisely so complicated that an *optimal* number of people join the programme. If this is not acceptable, society (the taxpayers) may have to carry the costs for some 'over-vaccination'.

The environment

There are also laws intended to protect public health by protecting the general environment. If you own a factory, you are not allowed to put the health of others in jeopardy by polluting the environment. Such laws may be defended in a manner that does not involve paternalism. The political authorities could prohibit pollution because it harms the health of, not the polluters themselves, but others.

However, this argument is not always effective. When dealing with such subjects as pollution, we must realise that there may exist a kind of threshold effect in the field. It may be correctly argued, in some cases, that while many agents *together* harm the environment and endanger public health, by each spreading some substance in the air, no *one* in particular causes any harm. Each may correctly argue that, if he or she abstained from spreading one substance, while the others continued spreading others, then, from the point of view of the health of the population, this would make no difference whatever. And, should he or she alone be spreading one substance, no harm would be done at all.

The point here is not that no *noticeable* difference is made by each individual spreading one substance. There may be sub-noticeable differences, and a person may be held responsible for making a sub-noticeable difference, or so I am prepared to argue.[7] The point is not epistemic, but ontological. The point is that, with respect to the health situation, there may be no difference *whatever*, either noticeable or sub-noticeable.

If this is true, if no one in particular threatens the health situation of the others, while many together do so, it is clear that we need a general prohibition. This prohibition is not paternalist, but it is still problematic from the point of view of the principle of respect for personal autonomy that I have stated in Chapter 2.

How can I defend someone being prohibited from doing something that does not harm anyone else? How can I defend such a prohibition while, at the same time, wanting to permit *other* people to do *considerable* harm to others? (The latter is something we have to tolerate in a civilised society. Society cannot effectively stop all kinds of harm to others. This is simply not *possible*. Not even a totalitarian society would be able to do this.)

What we need here is an idea to the effect that laws should be designed, not only to protect individuals from possible harm caused by individuals, but also, *to protect individuals from harm caused by collectivities*.

I am not quite sure whether J.S. Mill saw this complication, but perhaps he makes an indirect reference to it when he writes about interference with the liberty of an individual, based on the importance (to others) of maintaining a certain practice, i.e. if the interference was 'grounded on the direct interest which others have in each individual's observance of the practice' (Mill 1973: 222).

The workplace

An even more serious threat to the idea that personal autonomy be respected may seem to be provided by laws protecting the health and safety of employees at workplaces.

Obviously, such laws are needed. However, how can such laws be defended? After all, if employees agree to work under dangerous conditions, and are compensated economically for doing so, why should they not be allowed to do so?

As a matter of fact, I think they should be allowed to do so. There should be no laws forbidding them, in their own best interest, to accept a dangerous occupation. If they are informed about the risks, if they freely choose to accept them, they should be allowed to do so. To think otherwise would be to yield to an illegitimate form of paternalism.

However, the situation is very different with employers. There exists no corresponding right for them to offer dangerous jobs. How should laws prohibiting them from doing so be defended?

---

7 In *Hedonistic Utilitarianism* (1998: Chapter 4), I defend the notion and existence of sub-noticeable differences of wellbeing.

Here I feel that I need to dissociate myself from J.S. Mill. According to Mill, the individual is not allowed to harm other people, but the individual is allowed to act in a manner that means that others, *with their own free and informed consent*, may suffer harm. According to Mill, it would be an example of illegitimate paternalism to stop two contracting parties from agreeing to terms where one party pays the other for taking a certain risk.

> As soon as any part of a person's conduct affects prejudicially the interests of others, society has jurisdiction over it. . . . But there is no room for entertaining any such question when a person's conduct affects the interests of no persons beside himself, *or needs not affect them unless they like* (all the persons concerned being of full age, and the ordinary amount of understanding).
>
> (Mill 1973: 205–206, my emphasis)

I find this position *too* liberal. Instead I want to defend, in this field, a kind of well-behaved paternalism.

It *is* legitimate for society to *stop* one person from *allowing* another person (by hiring him or her, for example) to undergo harm, it seems to me. It is also legitimate for society to stop one person from putting others at risk, even if this occurs with their free consent. This is a kind of paternalism, with the interest of the third party in focus (society, S, stops an individual or collectivity, A, from allowing that an individual, B, be hurt, in the best interests of B), but it is a well-behaved and acceptable form of paternalism.

From a utilitarian point of view, this kind of well-behaved paternalism is not hard to defend. After all, from a utilitarian point of view it is only natural to take an inclusive view of responsibility. We are responsible, not only for the harm we do, but also for the harm we allow to take place. So why should not society be allowed to hold us accountable for it? It is hard to see why J.S. Mill, who *was* a utilitarian, did not adopt this line of argument.

However, from other moral points of view, what I call 'well-behaved' paternalism might seem more difficult to defend. I think in particular of certain libertarian ideas of *rights*, granting the individual exactly the *basic* right to involve others in practices that harm these people, provided these people freely agree to engage in such practices.

I take exception to these ideas, but it is beyond the scope of this book to discuss them any further. It must suffice here to note that, in this area there are thinkers who are prepared to go even *further* than the present author does, in giving licence to people in their dealings with political authorities. It should also be noted, however, that in all European countries, and even in the US, a principle of well-behaved paternalism is operative within the health care system. It is not permitted, for example, for a doctor to involve a patient in a clinical trial, where the risks far out-weigh the possible benefits, and blame his patient, if he or she is harmed. It does not matter that the patient was informed of the risks and under-took them voluntarily. The doctor will be held responsible for the harm caused to the patient all the same.

The distinction between 'ordinary' and 'well-behaved' paternalism is relevant also when it comes to society's legitimate reaction to such things as drugs and prostitution.

Drugs

In many Western countries there are all sorts of regulations intended to protect people against their own possible abuse of various different drugs (alcohol, narcotics, medicines and so forth).

To some extent such prohibitions are intended to protect *young* people, in their own best interest, from starting to use these drugs. And to some extent these laws reflect political precautions people voluntarily take against their *own* irrationality. This is not at variance with the principle of respect for personal autonomy that I have defended in Chapter 1 of this book.

However, to the extent that these laws and regulations are intended by the majority to protect a minority of grown-up and competent persons against their own possible abuse of drugs, the laws and regulations are problematic.

This does not mean that such laws could not legitimately be enacted, however. For the discussion in the foregoing two sections has prepared the ground for a kind of possible defence of them. The defence is complicated, but it is not obviously flawed. The defence is as follows.

It could be argued with some plausibility that, while some people can freely use some drugs, such as alcohol, without becoming addicted, others cannot. Now, the more people who use the drugs, and the more they use them, the more people will become addicted.

The point need not be that each person who uses a drug causes any harm in particular. The point could be that people who use drugs *together* cause the harm in question. So, if use is restricted by an act of law, the rationale of the law need not be that people be protected against their *own* use of the drug – but that those who together put others at risk should be restrained.

To this it might be objected that, even if some people, who cannot handle the drugs, become addicted, those who can handle them are not to blame. Individually they do not cause any harm and, even if together they do, those who are harmed are themselves to blame. No one has forced them to use the drugs. They use them of their own free will and therefore they should bear the full consequences of their misuse of them. It is not *fair* that people who can handle the drugs should have to abstain from doing so, or restrict their use, only because there are people who cannot handle the drugs.

Note, however, that if we accept the kind of well-behaved paternalism I defended in the previous section, then society can prohibit, legitimately, those who can handle the drugs, from doing so, in the best interest of those who cannot. Those who can handle the drugs, and do use them, do 'cause' harm, not individually, perhaps, but together, and in a sense relevant to morality (they are responsible, and they should be held accountable, for what they bring about). So when the political authorities prohibit those who can handle the drugs from using the drugs, they do not flout the principle of respect for personal autonomy.

This does not suffice to defend any kind of regulation in particular, of the use of any drug in particular, of course. It does suffice, however, to defend the claim that such regulations need not be at variance with the principle of respect for personal autonomy.

Perhaps there should be very *severe* such regulations (perhaps they save lives). Perhaps there should be *no* such regulations (perhaps they are ineffective, or even counterproductive). Solving this problem lies outside the scope of this book.

Prostitution

An argument similar to the one presented in my discussion of the regulation of drugs can be applied to prostitution. Unless it can be proved that prostitutes put their clients at risk, it would mean a violation of their rights to forbid them from doing their job. The fact that their choice of profession may cause harm to themselves is not a sufficient warrant for society to stop them from pursuing it (if they are competent and if they have reached the age of maturity). Moreover, to the extent that they are dangerous to their clients, they should be *punished* for the harm they do, rather than stopped from pursuing the career they have chosen. This is a theme to which I will return in chapters to come.

However, this does not mean that society must, if it wants to hold on to the principle of personal autonomy, tolerate prostitution. A case could be made for social legislation, not against prostitutes offering their services, but against their clients accepting their offers (and buying their services).

At first it might seem that such a prohibition would obviously flout the principle of respect for personal autonomy. Should not prostitutes *and* their clients, to the extent that they are competent and have reached the age of maturity, be free to make whatever contracts they see fit?

However, this need not be the case. The following kind of argument could be presented. When people buy sexual services from prostitutes, they collectively see to it that the 'profession' will continue to exist, as a possible choice for women (and some men). However, this is not a professional career that *should* exist, it could be argued. The career is much too risky. Those who become prostitutes put their lives in jeopardy in their dealings with their clients. Furthermore, the psychic traumas they are bound to suffer are considerable. Society cannot and does not tolerate health risks of this magnitude at workplaces in general, so it should not tolerate them in relation to prostitution. The clients are, in their relation to the prostitutes, in the same kind of relation that an employer is with respect to the employee. If we can stop the employer from putting the employee at risk, then we can stop clients from buying sexual services from prostitutes – in the interests of the prostitutes.

I do not say that my argument provides us with a sound rationale for a prohibition against people buying services from prostitutes. Perhaps there should be such a prohibition, perhaps not. It all depends, in the final analysis, on whether such a prohibition would do more good than harm. Some argue that it would have very good effects indeed. Others claim that it would be counterproductive. This is not the place to assess these arguments.

However, my argument does show that, while a prohibition against people selling sexual services *would* flout the principle of personal autonomy, a corresponding prohibition against the buying of sexual services need *not* involve any similar violation of the principle.

Could not a similar argument show that the prostitutes, together, constitute a threat to society? Can it not be shown that they threaten social morality, the status of the family, women's rights or something of the kind?

I think not. The number of arguments to this effect is legion. However, they all seem far-fetched, to put it politely, or moralistic, with a smell of bigotry, to put it bluntly.

So if there are good utilitarian reasons for prohibiting prostitution, there exists only one acceptable way of prohibiting it, without flouting the principle of personal autonomy. In that case, the buying, not the selling of sexual services, should be banned by society.

4

INFECTIOUS DISEASES

Infectious diseases such as cholera, plague, smallpox, yellow fever, rabies and exanthematic typhus used to plague our societies in the past. To some extent, modern, industrially developed countries like the western European ones, the US, Canada, Japan and Australia, have been liberated from these problems as some of the worst diseases have been eradicated. However, some new ones have developed in their place, such as HIV/AIDS, and it is obvious that, within the foreseeable future, the problem of how to handle such diseases will be with us, in western Europe, the US, Canada, Japan and Australia as elsewhere. And the liberal use of antibiotics has meant that some of the old diseases are returning in more sinister forms than ever.

Infectious diseases are not only a problem for those who suffer from them but a problem for society. Society has a right to protect those who are not infected from becoming infected. This may mean that those who are infected must accept some restrictions on their way of life. To the extent that these restrictions are intended to protect others, they cannot be denounced for being paternalist. And to the extent that (a) they do not take the form of coercive *care*, (b) are necessary to safeguard the health of others and (c) are administered in a way that does not flout the ideal of judicial security, these kinds of restrictions are mandatory. It is an obligation for society to provide them. However, it is far from obvious what *forms* such restrictions should take.

In this respect, there is nothing at all to be learnt from the Convention, which is silent on this matter. The European Convention does comment on it. However, very little can be learnt from its comment. In the European Convention it is stated, extremely bluntly:

> No one shall be deprived of his liberty save in the following cases and in accordance with a procedure prescribed by law:

> . . .

e) the lawful detention of persons for the prevention of the spreading of infectious diseases, of persons of unsound mind, alcoholics or drug addicts or vagrants . . .

(Article 5:1)

The European Convention, it seems to me, gives the authorities much too much room for licence in the treatment of people who suffer from infectious diseases. Moreover, the paragraph is prejudicial in a very nasty manner, in that it treats people suffering from infectious diseases together with people 'of unsound mind' and 'vagrants', whatever that may mean. As a matter of fact, I must confess that I was really shocked to find this paragraph, so flagrantly at variance with the ideal of judicial security, included in the document at all.

The actual legal situation for people suffering from, or carrying, communicable infectious diseases, is also very varied in Europe. In relation to HIV/AIDS, a special recommendation was made by the Committee of Ministers of the Council of Europe, on 24 October 1989 (No. R (89) 14). This is a highly enlightened document. It is so enlightened that the country that treats people with HIV/AIDS most harshly, Sweden, had to abstain from voting for it, making an explanatory statement saying that the Swedish government will not consider itself bound by the recommendation. Iceland, too, had some problems with this recommendation. And in some states in the US, harsh practices have existed as well. Although bitter opposition greeted all attempts to bring dangerous behaviour of HIV-infected people within the scope of existing quarantine statutes, more than a dozen states did so from 1987 through 1990 (Bayer 1991).

The question to be discussed in the present chapter is: how *should* society react to people with communicable infectious diseases? In particular, how should society react when people carrying infectious diseases pose a threat to other people? What kind of measures taken against these people are compatible with the ideal of non-paternalism as well as the ideal of judicial security?

May society impose lifestyle rules?

It is obvious that society must be allowed to restrict the lifestyle of people carrying dangerous infectious diseases, even sexually transmitted diseases such as HIV/AIDS. The nature of the restrictions must depend, ultimately, on the nature of the disease and on how easily it is spread.

HIV/AIDS is a very serious (lethal) disease but, luckily enough, a disease that is not easily spread. The modes of HIV transmission are limited to sexual intercourse, mingling of blood and the mother-to-foetus relation. This means that the restrictions on lifestyle concerning people who carry the disease need not be very far-reaching.

81

It is important that people who are infected inform sexual partners about this, before any intercourse takes place. It is also important that people who may come in contact with the blood of infected people are informed about the danger. Pregnant women who are HIV infected may come to consider abortion. However, it is far from obvious that abortion is what a woman must seek, if she has the best interests of her future child as her main concern.

To be sure, the mother-to-be may come to die, leaving her child orphaned. And the child may come to be born infected. It is far more likely that the child will be born without the infection than with it, however. And there may be another parent (the father) to take full responsibility, if the mother dies. And, most important of all, from the point of view of the future child, even if it is infected, the choice of the mother means a life as infected (if she carries her pregnancy to term) or no life at all (if she chooses abortion). It is far from obvious that a life with the HIV infection is so grim that a person who is living it must regret that he or she was born at all.

Would it be acceptable to go even further? Could society demand that people who are HIV positive abstain from sex, or confine themselves to safe sex?

I think this would be acceptable, though it may seem to run counter to the ideal of anti-paternalism. If a person has been informed that his or her sexual partner is HIV positive and yet, for all that, consents to having unsafe sex with him or her, then this person is him- or herself to blame, it could be thought. Society should not stop this person from taking the risk, if this is what he or she wants to do.

My answer to this argument should be clear from my discussion about drugs, prostitution and other subjects in Chapter 2. I agree that no one should he stopped from having unprotected sex with a HIV-positive person, if the intercourse takes place with informed consent. To stop anyone from doing this would be to act, in an illegitimate sense of the word, 'paternalistically' with respect to this person. However, I do not think it would be paternalistic of society to forbid the HIV-positive person from putting the other person at risk, even if this took place on a voluntary and fully informed basis. In my defence of the anti-paternalist ideal, I do want to make room for this kind of well-behaved paternalism.

The reason for making room for this kind of well-behaved paternalism, we recall, was that, after all, we *are* morally responsible for the consequences of our actions, and for the harm we do – even if it comes about through the free consent of another human being. But then society may well hold us responsible for them.

The upshot of this is that society may well make it an act of law that no one who knows that he or she is HIV positive should be allowed to have unprotected sex with a person who is not HIV positive, with or without the informed consent of this person. However, it might be too radical to have a law forbidding HIV-positive people to become prostitutes (as is the case in Austria, see Mann and Fluss 1989: 19). It should suffice to forbid prostitutes who are HIV positive from having unprotected sex. And, of course, they should be obliged to inform their customers of their condition.

Now, the nature of HIV/AIDS means that such a prohibition, together with a sound social strategy with respect to information, education, testing and treatment on a voluntary basis, would probably suffice to counter the threat from this infection. However, what if an even worse disease were to emerge?

There is in principle no limit to how narrowly society may restrict the life of a person infected by a serious disease, if the disease is lethal and is spread very easily. One can imagine diseases such that, if a person were infected by them, he or she would have to emigrate immediately to some remote quarantine. If this very strict regulation was indeed the only means to save others from the disease, there would be no objection to it. In particular, it would not thwart the principle of respect for the autonomy of the individual in decisions about medical care and social services.

Severe restrictions on people's lifestyle may be warranted by the nature of the infectious disease they carry, then. In principle, there is no limit to how harsh the restrictions may have to become. This is determined by the dangerousness of the disease (and the dangerousness of the disease is, so to speak, the product of the probability that it be communicated and the severity of it).

However, what about those who do not abide by these restrictions? How is society supposed to react to them?

May society detain people who put others at risk?

If society has stated, for example, through an act of law, that no one who is infected with a certain disease is allowed to have unprotected sexual intercourse with any other person who is not infected with the disease in question, and a person has been found to violate this law, then this person could be prosecuted and punished for his or her criminal offence. This is how society *ought* to react, when its laws are transgressed. However, in relation to infectious disease, would this be sufficient?

It might be tempting to argue in the following manner. When a person has been convicted of having infected other persons with a disease it may be too late for society to react. If the disease is sexually transmitted, it might be difficult to prove that the crime has actually taken place. The victim may be reluctant to come forward and so the criminal person may continue his or her dangerous behaviour for a long time. Would it not be better if society could single out infectious persons with a lifestyle that is in more general ways likely, in combination with the infection, to produce danger to other persons? Would it not be acceptable for society to detain, for example, HIV-positive prostitutes, even if it could not actually be proved that they had had unprotected sex with any client? By the time this can be proved, many innocent persons, in particular, many innocent wives of the men that visit these prostitutes, may have been infected.

A law to the effect that HIV-positive prostitutes could be compulsorily detained would be in line, it seems to me, with the European Convention and its provision about 'the lawful detention of persons for the prevention of the spreading of infectious diseases'. And yet, I think we ought to resist this line of argument. It is also at variance with the spirit of the afore-mentioned recommendation made by the Council of Europe.

My reluctance to accept it, and my reasons for disliking the system prac-tised in Sweden to this effect (and the system practised in some states of the US) is based on the ideal of judicial security. In two important ways, laws making room for the detention of people with infectious disease and a 'dangerous' lifestyle may come to be at variance with this ideal.

First, it may well be argued, if society rules that infectious people with a dangerous lifestyle be compulsorily detained, then the obvious risk is that only people who are for other reasons stigmatised in society will be the ones who are detained. This is what has happened in Sweden, where a law gives the authorities much licence with respect to HIV-positive people. Those who are detained are street prostitutes, drug addicts and black Africans. This does not mean that there are no other people who exhibit a 'dangerous' lifestyle. However, to the extent that they are well integrated in society, they do not get detained.

To this it might perhaps be replied that the problematic aspect of this is not that prostitutes, drug addicts and black Africans are detained, but that other people with a similarly dangerous lifestyle are *not* detained. A similar argument has been given with respect to capital punishment in the US. When confronted with statistics showing that black people are over-represented on the death rows, in particular if they have been convicted for having murdered white people, some advocates of capital punishment have answered that what is problematic about this is not that black people get executed but that white people don't (van den Haag 1991).

There is something to this argument. However, if it turns out to be posi-tively impossible in the US to execute white people, who have killed black people, then the argument from judicial security informs us that, no matter how good the reasons that can otherwise be given for capital punishment, capital punishment must remain highly problematic.

I will not go any further into the discussion about capital punishment here (there are no good arguments for it, I believe). However, it seems obvious to me that, with respect to detention of people who are HIV posi-tive and have a dangerous lifestyle, it is indeed impossible to reach those who are well established in society. Moreover, it is a definite risk that people who do not really live a 'dangerous' lifestyle at all will be falsely believed to do so simply because there are such strong prejudices already against people such as prostitutes, drug addicts and, in western European countries, black Africans. The argument from the ideal of judicial security therefore informs us that no such detention should take place, even if, in principle, it would be an acceptable way of handling the problem with the danger posed by the disease in question.

Second, and even more important, the detention of infected people with a dangerous lifestyle is not an acceptable way of handling the problem of the danger posed by infectious diseases at all. If people who have not 'yet' been convicted for having committed the crime of threatening the life and safety of other persons are to be detained, this must be on predictive grounds. A prediction must be made to the effect that these people are more likely than other people to come to pose a threat to others. Well, I suppose the prediction must go further than that. It must really be predicted that these people will, as a matter of fact, come to pose a threat to other persons. Otherwise it would be a kind of judicial crime to detain infected people with dangerous lifestyles. However, there are no scientific resources available that render such predictions possible.

Many mistaken predictions will be made. There will be both 'false positives' and 'false negatives'. The false negatives will reduce the efficiency of the system. The false positives will have even more serious effects. They will mean that people in general cannot feel safe in their dealings with authorities any longer. People in general will not know how to behave, in order not to be detained. Certain groups of people in particular, such as homosexuals, will feel that they cannot trust the authorities.

All this may, if the worst comes to the worst, mean a total breakdown of the vulnerable 'social contract', providing the European states as well as the US, Canada, Japan and Australia with a reasonable degree of political order and stability.

May society coercively treat people who break the rules?

I have argued against the idea that people carrying an infectious disease and exhibiting a 'dangerous' lifestyle should be on that ground detained. However, I have accepted that people should be punished (and sentenced to gaol) for having knowingly spread an infectious disease to others (even if this took place with the informed consent of those who became infected). This means that I must face the question of how society should react to infected people who have been detained (who are in prison because of their crime). Would it be all right for society coercively to try to change the lifestyle of these people? In spite of the fact that this is standard procedure in many countries, this is not acceptable, it seems to me.

It is *obvious* that people who are detained on the ground that they follow a dangerous lifestyle should not be coercively treated against their choice of lifestyle. They should not have been detained in the first place. It is less obvious, of course, that people who have been convicted for having posed a threat to the life and health of others should not be coerced to accept treatment against their selected lifestyle. However, even in this case society ought to abstain from coercion, it seems to me.

These people should be offered help in changing their callous way of life. When the time comes to decide about parole or a shortening of their punishment, it is perfectly legitimate to take into consideration whether these people have or have not accepted the suggested treatment (if such a treatment exists) and to what extent it has proved successful. When people are granted parole or have their sentences shortened it is perfectly legiti- mate to make an assessment of how dangerous they may (still) be. This is well in accordance with the ideal of judicial security. However, if a person does not want to accept such an offer of treatment, he or she should be free to serve his or her time instead.

The reasons for this stance will be spelt out more fully in Chapter 6, dealing with forensic psychiatric care. Suffice it to say here that, unless a sharp demarcation is made between punishment and care, there is a defi- nite risk that the trust in the health care system will be undermined.

Such loss of the trust in the health care system means not only a loss of confidence in general, in society, with respect to the health care system, but also, in many situations, a loss in terms of efficiency in the care given. When it comes to therapies aimed at changing the behaviour (or even per- sonality) of a person, it is of crucial importance that the point of departure for the therapy be the active wish of the person treated to undergo the change in question.

Compulsory testing

A much discussed question is whether society should ever make testing for infectious diseases compulsory.

I see no principled reason why this should not take place. It should take place, it seems to me, if the disease is highly dangerous and highly conta- gious (so that it is practically impossible for infected people not to infect others). This means that people singled out for testing can be singled out on 'objective' grounds. Those who live in an area where the disease has been spread, or those who travel through such an area, and so forth, may be subjected to compulsory testing. Moreover, people who donate blood, organs or tissue, *ought to* be tested for infectious diseases such as HIV/ AIDS and hepatitis, since these diseases are transmitted together with blood.

This is perhaps not controversial. However, what about diseases that are dangerous but less contagious, so that the infected person him- or herself can take precautions against infecting others? Should people who are likely to carry such diseases and who exhibit a dangerous lifestyle be compulsorily tested, even if they do not volunteer as donors of blood, organs or tissue?

It should be obvious from the foregoing that my answer to this question is no. There is no way to single out the group in question on merely *predictive* grounds, that is not based partly, at least, on prejudice, and does not therefore flout the ideal of judicial security.

My answer is in this respect fully in accordance with the aforementioned recommendation from the Council of Europe, which states:

> – in the light of present knowledge and in the absence of curative treatment, [we] consider systematic screening unethical and contrary to the rights of individuals, if carried out automatically on population groups without informed consent and without counselling, because it overrides the principles of autonomy and physical integrity, affects the privacy of the individual, and is likely to have serious psychological, social and financial consequences for the individual.
>
> (No. R (89) 14: IAa)

However, this does not mean that society must be complacent when people put others at risk. If such behaviour has been forbidden, through an act of law, then a criminal charge can be brought against these people. If they are found guilty as charged, then they can be convicted for what they have actually done (not for what they are likely to do).

Suppose one person accuses another of having put him or her at risk, through unprotected sex. A strong suspicion exists that this is what has actually taken place and that, as a matter of fact, this person carries an infectious disease that is dangerous and sexually transmitted. The suspicion is so strong that a criminal investigation is undertaken. Now, as part of this investigation, the accused person may well be compulsorily tested. This is no different from what happens in paternity cases.

Of course, this is an intrusion into the privacy of this person. But such intrusions are part and parcel of the system of criminal justice, where even innocent persons are held in custody, waiting for a trial that will, perhaps, acquit them of all accusations. These persons may have to undergo various kinds of testing, they must give their finger prints and so forth. This is the price these persons have to pay for a system we all need.

Of course, if some person who has been held in custody and compulsorily tested for a certain disease, is found innocent, we ought to *compensate* him or her, as far as is possible, for the harm he or she has suffered. And if he or she is found guilty, the time in custody should be deducted from the punishment he or she receives.

Conclusion

To conclude this chapter: society ought to fight the spread of infectious diseases. The struggle against these diseases should take place first and foremost in the form of information, education and positive encouragement. People should be informed about the risks, educated about ways of countering them, and encouraged to take all the necessary precautions.

If the disease is dangerous and if it is highly contagious, society may go even further than that. When fighting a dangerous infectious disease, which is easily spread, it is perfectly justifiable for society to restrict the life and habits of people infected by the disease in question. Compulsory testing, when the group to be tested can be selected on objective grounds, is not objectionable as such. The scope and limits of these restrictions and obligations should be determined solely by how dangerous the disease is and how easily it is being spread.

When people infected with a disease do not abide by the rules society has stipulated, through its acts of law, these people should be convicted for their crimes and punished. No other kind of reaction, such as preventive detention of people who are infected and exhibit a 'dangerous lifestyle', is legitimate for society to adopt. Neither should compulsory testing of people in 'risk groups' take place. These people should instead be encouraged to seek testing on a voluntary basis, respecting their privacy, and they should get all the help they may need to change their lifestyle voluntarily.

Even while keeping an infected person in gaol, society should offer this person all possible help to change his or her lifestyle. However, no coercive care should take place.

If it is the decision taken by this person, he or she should be allowed to reject all kinds of treatment, serving, instead, his or her full time for the crime committed.

5

MENTAL ILLNESS

In all Western countries there are laws regulating the compulsory admission of mentally ill people. Most countries have *specific* mental health legislations. Countries in Europe which do not have such legislation are Albania, Croatia, Iceland, Lithuania, Poland, Romania, Slovenia, Spain and Turkey (Jensen 1994: 10). However, considerable differences exist between Western countries. Here are some examples.

In the US involuntary hospitalisation occurs through the legal process of civil commitment. The legal process and the standard for commitment are broadly similar in all fifty states. Civil commitment is seen as a deprivation of liberty. Therefore, the law requires that a clear police power or *parens patriae* state interest be involved (Beck 1996: 12).

In some European countries, such as England and Wales and Russia, health care personnel decide about the compulsory admission and there are no proceedings in court.

In the Netherlands the Mayor of the municipality has the power to order a mentally ill person to be kept in hospital for up to six days. A doctor must certify the need for compulsory admission. If the patient cannot be released after six days it is necessary to obtain a decision from the court. The compulsory admission can last for six months, and it can be prolonged by the court.[1]

In Germany, only the local court can order compulsory admission of a patient.[2]

In Spain the health care authorities can make decisions about compulsory admission. If the patient is detained in an institution a judge must be notified within twenty-four hours. The judge either authorises the compulsory admission or refuses authorisation and the judge is obliged to

1 The information in this chapter about the legal situation in England and Wales, the Netherlands, Spain and Sweden, is gathered from Tor Sverne, 'Comments on the Legislation Concerning Impaired Capacity and Decision-Making in the Health Care Field in England and Wales, the Netherlands, Spain, and Sweden' (1997: 5–6).
2 I owe this and other information about Germany to Wulf Rössler *et al.* 'Changing Patterns of Mental Health Care in Germany' (1996).

review the situation of the patient at least every six months. In non-urgent cases the decision over compulsory admission is taken by a judge.

In Sweden health care personnel can issue a compulsory admission order. However, the senior consultant in the hospital must, within four weeks, apply to the administrative court for permission to continue the care for up to four months. After that the court can permit compulsory admission for up to six months, and so on.

Another difference between countries is over the medical treatment of mental illness during the compulsory admission. Here again are some examples.

In the US medication against the will of a competent patient is not permitted. When a patient is not competent a court will take a decision about medication. Typically, the standard considered appropriate to decide whether to medicate an incompetent patient is substituted judgement: what the patient would have decided if competent. This is explicit in *Rogers* v. *Commissioner of Dept of Mental Health* (458 N.E. 2d 308–323, 1983) (see Beck 1996: 14).

In England and Wales medical treatment for the mental disease can be given without consent in cases of committal for more than 72 hours.

In the Netherlands medical treatment without consent is permitted only if the patient causes a danger that cannot be avoided without such treatment.

In Spain and Sweden health care personnel can give the patient medical treatment without consent during a compulsory admission.

This rich variety of practices is allowed for in Article 7 of the previously mentioned Convention on Human Rights and Biomedicine, adopted by the Committee of Ministers in the Council of Europe on 19 November 1996, which states:

> Subject to protective conditions prescribed by law, including supervisory, control, and appeal procedures, a person who has a mental disorder of a serious nature may be subjected, without his or her consent, to an intervention aimed at treating his or her mental disorder only where, without such treatment, serious harm is likely to result to his or her health.

In this paragraph, it should be observed, it is stated that coercive care *may* be given to people who have a mental disorder of a serious nature; it is not stated that such people *must* be compulsorily admitted; it is taken for granted that each state may arrange the admission as it sees fit, provided the procedure is regulated by law (including supervisory control and appeal procedures).

This licence granted by the Convention means that, in many countries, a person can be compulsorily admitted as soon as he or she is in need of treatment, does not consent to the treatment, and where no better alternative exists (this is the case in countries like Italy and Sweden, for example).[3] In other countries a criterion of 'acute danger to the self or others' is stipulated (this is the case in Austria and Germany).

Note however that in the quoted paragraph it is explicitly stated that coercive treatment may only be given if, without such treatment, serious harm is likely to result *to the health of the patient*; it must not be given in the interest of *other* people (such as close relatives, or the public at large). In this the paragraph differs from what is stipulated in an earlier recommendation (No. R (83) 2) adopted by the Committee of Ministers of the Council of Europe on 22 February 1983, entitled 'Legal Protection of Persons Suffering from Mental Disorder Placed as Involuntary Patients'. According to Article 3 of this recommendation, 'a patient may be placed in an establishment only when, by reason of his mental disorder, he represents a serious danger to himself *or to other persons*'.

Many actual laws in the US and in European countries are at variance with this new requirement of the Convention. This is the case with the otherwise rather restrictive German law, for example, as well as the law in many US states. I will return to this point.

Three main questions come to mind when this brief overview of the actual international situation is undertaken. I will discuss them in order.

First, we have the question of on what grounds people *should* be coercively treated for mental illness. In the Convention it is stated that people with a serious mental disorder may be subjected without consent to an intervention aimed at treating his or her mental disorder. However, nothing is said about *when* this kind of intervention *ought* to take place. Nothing is said, in particular, about the *grounds* on which it should take place.

This provides much licence for the countries that may come to adopt the Convention. They may have a law setting out very strict rules, allowing only that *some* people suffering from a serious mental disorder be coercively treated for their disorder, or they may have a law stipulating simply that *all* persons who have a serious mental disorder and need medical intervention aimed at treating this mental disorder be treated, with or without their consent. The question to be discussed here is: on what grounds *should* people be submitted to coercive treatment for their mental illness?

Second, we have the question of who should decide. Should the doctors decide, in conformity with the aforementioned British model? Or, should a judge make the decision, in conformity with the German or Dutch model? Or, should there be a combination, in conformity with the Spanish or Swedish model?

---

3 I owe this information about Italy to Lorenzo Burti and Paul R. Benson, 'Psychiatric Reform in Italy' (1996).

Finally, we have the question of medication. Should the doctors be free, as they see fit, to medicate people against their will, as soon as these people have been compulsorily admitted to a mental hospital? Or, should there be special rules regulating the medication of these patients?

On what grounds should coercive care be given?

Three main ideas deserve discussion. First, it could be held, people suffering from a mental illness, who need medical treatment for it, and who do not assent to the treatment, should be coercively treated for their illness.

This is a model which takes advantage of *all* the scope for coercion allowed for by the Convention. I will refer to it as the Need Model. This model is followed, in an informal way, in Russia, England and Wales and, in a more formalised way, in countries like Sweden, Spain and Italy. In most US states involuntary hospitalisation or treatment can only take place if a person is both mentally ill and dangerous to him- or herself or others. However, in recent years, seven states have expanded the definiton of *parens patriae*. Those states permit civil commitment of *non-dangerous* persons who are severely ill or in need of treatment or incompetent to decide about hospital treatment (Beck 1996: 13).

Both Swedish and Italian law stress the fact that it is solely the need of the patient that warrants commitment, not the interests of other people. The other countries mentioned here use the Need Model but go beyond it in committing people who are dangerous to others *as well*. This is true of the US. The Russian law is special in that it allows that people be committed on the grounds of 'helplessness', as well as on strict *medical* grounds (mental illness) (Jensen 1994: 12).

Second, a more restricted model would be that only people who suffer from mental illness, who need medical treatment for it, whose lives are put at risk if they are not treated and who do not assent to the treatment, should be coercively treated for their illness. I will refer to this as the Life Rescue Model.

Finally, a third model would be the following: only people who suffer from mental illness, who need medical treatment for it, who are not capable of making an autonomous decision about their medical needs and who do not assent to the treatment, should be coercively treated for their illness. I will refer to this as the Incompetency Model.

The Incompetency Model is not practised in any country or state I know of, even if some US states use the reference to incompetency as one criterion among others. However, in contradistinction to the Need Model, it is compatible with the Declaration of Hawaii, where the following is stated:

No procedure shall be performed nor treatment given against or independent of a patient's own will, unless because of mental illness, the patient cannot form a judgement as to what is in his or her own best interest and without which treatment serious impairment is likely to occur to the patient or others.

(Article 5)

These three models, the Need Model, the Life Rescue Model and the Incompetency Model, do not exhaust all logical possibilities, but they constitute the three most promising ideas in the field. Clearly, they use different criteria for compulsory admission. However, do they also differ in practice?

I think it obvious that the Life Rescue Model allows for less coercion than the Need Model in practice. This is hardly controversial. However, what about the Need Model as compared to the Incompetency Model? Are there *actual* cases where people suffer from mental illness, need medical treatment for their illness, do not assent to the treatment, but are capable of making a autonomous decision?

It is hard (for a lay man) to tell how often this is the case but, it seems to me, there are indeed some actual cases of the kind. If we reject the Life Rescue Model (as I believe we should), we must choose between the Need model and the Incompetency Model – a choice of the utmost importance as it is not only a matter of how coercion is motivated (an important question as such) but also a matter of who should be, and who should not be, coerced.

The second model, the Life Rescue Model, which comes close to what is practised in Germany (the difference between this model and the one practised in Germany is that the risk a person's mental illness may pose to *other* persons is also a legitimate ground for compulsory admission in Germany, but not in this model; I will return to this later on), does not strike me as acceptable. The Life Rescue Model might seem superior to the much too inclusive Need Model but it appears too restrictive when compared to the Incompetency Model.

If a treatment exists, if a person needs it, but cannot make an autonomous decision, then it would be wrong not to coerce this person into accepting the treatment in question, irrespective of the grounds for the incompetency of this person.

Coercively treating this person is not at variance with the principle of respect for the autonomy of the individual in decisions about medical care and social services. When such coercion is exercised, it is reasonable to assume that the coerced person, if capable of making an autonomous decision, would assent to it.

It follows from this that the Incompetency Model ought to be adopted, in spite of the fact that, to my knowledge, it is not being practised in any country or state.

93

There are three major arguments in favour of the Incompetency Model. First, of the three models, only the Incompetency Model is compatible with the principle of respect for the autonomy of the individual in decisions about medical care and social services, as stated and defended in Chapter 1. Second, as compared to the Need Model the Incompetency Model is better because it is compatible with the Declaration of Hawaii while the Need Model is not. And, finally, as compared with the Life Rescue Model, the Incompetency Model allows us to rescue the health of a person who cannot make an autonomous decision about his or her need of health care. The Life Rescue Model does not permit this unless the threat to the health of this person is so grave that, if he or she is not helped, he or she will actually *die*.

All this creates a strong presumption for the adoption of the Incompetency Model.

However, it might be thought that, while it is reasonable to abide by the principle of respect for the autonomy of the individual in decisions about medical care and social services in relation to somatic health care, the principle cannot be applied to mental illness. Mental illness is different, it might be held. Mentally ill persons must also be guarded against their own *autonomous* decisions. Mentally ill persons do not know their own best interests. With respect to mentally ill persons, only the Need Model is justifiable.

For all its popularity, we ought to resist this argument. It might be argued of course that, unless we protect mentally ill persons against their misapprehensions of their situation, even when they are capable of exercising an autonomous decision, they will harm themselves. They do not know their own best interests. For example, unless we stop some of them, they will give away everything they own, or, unless we lock up others among them, they will kill themselves: if we protect all these people from harming themselves we help them to sustain a prosperous and perhaps long life, once they are cured of their illness. In the future, they may even themselves come to thank us for having done so.

This is not convincing. At least in a civilised society, a person should be allowed to give away all his or her property, and yet, for all that, live a decent life. If necessary, the social services should see to this.

And a person capable of exercising an autonomous decision ought to be allowed to kill him- or herself (even if the suicide need not be a physician-assisted one – I put that question to one side in the present chapter). After all, even if mentally ill, he or she has a privileged position when it comes to judging the value of his or her life. And no one, at least no doctor or social worker, has any stake in the outcome that competes with the person's own.

However, what if the person in question has a very *strange* view of reality? What if he or she falsely believes, for example, that the CIA has taken control of psychiatric care? What if he or she absurdly claims that the CIA has mixed arsenic with the medicine administered on the psychiatric ward? Are not these beliefs so bizarre that it would be wrong to accept decisions based on them?

They are nothing of the kind, it seems to me. They are no more bizarre than the religious belief, entertained by a member of Jehovah's Witnesses, to the effect that, should he or she accept a blood transfusion, he or she will end up in Hell.

As a matter of fact, if *I* were given the information that, unexpectedly, *one* of these two beliefs – either the belief that the CIA had taken control of psychiatric care, or the belief that if I accepted a blood transfusion, I would end up in Hell – was true, I would bet that it was the one to the effect that the CIA had taken control of psychiatric care that was true!

So if we accept that members of Jehovah's Witnesses may refuse blood transfusions, which we should do, or so I have argued in Chapter 2 at any rate, then, on grounds of judicial security, we cannot deny mentally ill persons an equal right to refuse treatment of their mental illness.

Does all this mean that mentally ill persons should *never* be treated against their will? It does not. They should be treated, if they need treatment, refuse to give their consent to it *and are incapable of making an autonomous decision about the treatment.*

Not all mental illness incapacitates (all the time). However, some mental illness does (sometimes) incapacitate the person suffering from it. This is probably the case with most people who refuse treatment because they believe that the CIA has taken control of the psychiatric care. Their decision should not be discounted because it is based on a highly *implausible* hypothesis. It may be discounted, however, because it is based on beliefs that have a compulsive character – if this is actually the case. In particular it should be discounted if the person in question is not capable of revising his or her beliefs in the light of new arguments or experiences.

This is not to say that the person in question must *actually* revise his or her beliefs, if new arguments or experiences are forthcoming. The crucial thing is that the person in question *can* do this. He or she may well refuse to do so.

As was noted in Chapter 1, this refusal to adopt the canons of sound reasoning is something most of us do, at some point, even when making very crucial decisions. We hold stubbornly to our own favoured beliefs and values. We are not, simply because of this, coerced by society into a socially desirable behaviour. But if *we* (who are not mentally ill) are not thus coerced, neither should mentally ill persons be thus coerced (any longer), once *they* have reached a state of mind where they are *capable* of exercising their autonomous judgement.

The upshot of this is that a person who is in the grips of an acute psychosis may be treated, against his or her will, for the psychosis. However, once the acute psychosis is over, and he or she can make an autonomous decision, he or she should be allowed to decide autonomously whether to go on with the treatment or not.

This person should even be allowed to commit suicide, if this is the option chosen. A mentally ill person may have very good reasons indeed to commit suicide.

The needs of others

Note that the needs of others are not allowed to play any role in the decision to admit a person to coercive care, according to the Convention. However, in many countries the needs of others *are* allowed to play some role. So these countries will have to change their laws, or make a reservation in respect of this provision of the Convention, when the Convention is approved of, accepted or ratified, or they will have to refer to Article 26 of the Convention, allowing for restrictions on the exercise of the rights defined in the Convention.

For example, in the Netherlands, the Psychiatric Patients Act allows that people suffering from mental illness which causes a danger to themselves or anyone else, a danger which cannot be averted by help outside the psychiatric hospital, be compulsorily admitted. And we have seen that this is the case also in Austria and Germany.

In France, furthermore, committal can be decided on by the Prefect of Police, on the grounds that the mentally ill person is a danger to him- or herself or others, *or to public order* (Jensen 1994: 11). (And even in a country like Sweden, where reference to the needs of others has been eliminated from the explicit statement of the law in question, it has been smuggled back into it; when the medical needs of the patient are to be assessed, it is stated in the law, some attention may after all be paid to whether the person in question is dangerous to others. If he or she is dangerous to others, then this is taken to indicate that he or she *needs* to be treated. This is not convincing.)

Moreover, in countries where people have committed crimes for which they *cannot* be punished (because in these countries the criminal law excuses people who have committed crimes under the influence of a serious mental disorder or illness, declares them unfit for trial, and so prohibits their being punished for what they have done), there simply *have* to be ways of detaining them.

All this means that it is not easy for the member states to live up to this particular provision of the Convention. Yet, for all that, I think the Convention *should* be upheld. This requires a radical reform of *the entire system* of handling those who are considered to be 'dangerously insane', however.

We will see in the next chapter how people who commit crimes under the influence of mental illness can be handled, without flouting the Convention. They should be put in prison rather than compulsorily admitted to psychiatric care, I suggest.

What about the rest, then, those who have not committed any crime, but who are simply considered a danger to other people (such as the members of their family)?

These people should not be treated against their will. There must be other ways to protect the relatives of mentally ill (and dangerous) persons. Mainly, this should take place through the active intervention of the social services, giving help and support to the relatives, encouraging them to file reports about what has taken place and so forth, and, in the final analysis, through the application of criminal law (of which I say more in the next chapter).

It should also be noted that there is no simple correlation between mental illness and criminal behaviour. As a matter of fact, it is extremely difficult to *predict* dangerous behaviour. If people are coercively treated for their mental illness, because they are considered dangerous, the prediction that they may cause harm may well be wrong. If we make rash judgements in this context, we flout the ideal of judicial security (see, for example, Menzies 1989; Monahan 1981; Webster and Menzies 1987).

Moreover, the fact that patients are treated on this ground, and not because of their own need, if this is allowed, may tempt psychiatry not to give them the treatment they need, but rather the treatment their relatives and their society need (i.e. treatment that makes them incapable of committing crimes rather than treatment that makes them unwilling to commit crimes).

And even if this is not actually the case, a *suspicion* that it is may be engendered, if people are treated not only for their own sake but also for the sake of others, and this suspicion may be difficult to eliminate effectively. This, in turn, may well give rise to an important therapeutic loss.

If the patient feels that he or she is treated, not for his or her own sake, but for the sake of others, and if he or she suspects that the treatment given is not really in his or her own best interest, he or she may hesitate to cooperate in the treatment. And the active cooperation of the patient is of crucial importance in therapeutic situations in general and, of course, in therapy for mental illness in particular.

We have very good reasons to try to abide by the Convention, then, in spite of the fact that this is rarely done. As will be shown in the next chapter, contrary to what is often taken for granted, this is not only a desirable, but also a possible stance for society to take up.

Who should decide?

The restrictive, Incompetency Model should be selected, then. According to this model, only people who suffer from mental illness, who need medical treatment for it, who are not capable of making an autonomous decision about their medical needs and who do not assent to the treatment, should be coercively treated for their illness. Preferably, the model should be incorporated in a revised version of the Convention. But who is to make the decisions about compulsory admittance?

In situations of emergency, doctors should make the decision. This is fairly obvious. However, their decisions should somehow be supervised. And the question remains: who should decide about compulsory committal once the emergency situation is over?

This decision, as well as the supervision of the emergency decision, should be taken by an administrative court, it seems to me. The doctor has a role to play when the decision is taken; not as the one responsible for the decision, however, but rather as an expert providing expert advice.

The doctor acting as an expert in court should not be the same doctor who is responsible for the treatment of the patient. This is to avoid conflicting roles.

The doctor functioning as an expert in court may plead that a certain person be compulsorily committed (to a closed ward in a psychiatric hospital), because of a mental illness making an autonomous decision impossible for this person. Such a judgement may offend the patient and be detrimental to the patient's trust in *his* or *her* doctor. So it is better that the doctor in question *not* be his or her doctor.

Why should the decision be taken by an administrative court, and not by a doctor? The reason is that the judgement whether a person is capable of making an autonomous decision is not a medical one as such. Medical information may be relevant to this judgement, but medical information in itself is not sufficient grounds for the judgement. This should be clear from how the notion of an autonomous will was defined in Chapter 1.

Actually, while there are experts on some of the factors that may make a person incapable of reaching an autonomous decision, such as mental illness, there are no experts on the question as such of whether a certain person is capable of exercising an autonomous will or not. So the reason why a judge should take the decision is not that a judge is an *expert* in the field in question but simply because *someone* has to take the decision. It is standard procedure to have a judge taking the decision, paying due respect to all relevant considerations. This is a way of seeing to it that the decision be impartial, well informed, public, and hence open to criticism.

Having a judge make the decision prepares the ground for a strict observance of the ideal of judicial security. The person who is compulsorily committed can be aided by a competent attorney, he or she can be informed about the grounds for the claim that he or she be committed to psychiatric treatment, he or she may have the possibility of obtaining a second medical opinion, he or she should have the right to a habeas corpus hearing and so forth.

Under these circumstances, people *should* sometimes, in their own best interests, be compulsorily committed to psychiatric care. For society *not* to treat them would be for society to fall victim to callous complacency.

And treating them, on the very strict grounds now stipulated, in the manner here indicated, is well in accordance with both the principle of non-paternalism and the ideal of judicial security. They are coercively treated on the plausible presumption that, if they could have reached an autonomous decision, they themselves would have opted for the treatment. Mental disease is no different from somatic disease in this respect. Most people who suffer from disease want professional help to get cured or, if this is not possible, to have palliative measures taken.

The role of the next of kin

In most European countries the next of kin are responsible for drawing attention to the necessity of committing a severely mentally ill person who is in need of treatment or is a danger to self or others. In some countries a signed, written request is required (Jensen 1994: 13). Does this constitute an acceptable practice?

It is not objectionable, it seems to me, that the next of kin are responsible for drawing attention to the necessity of committing a severely mentally ill person. We should *all* be obliged, it seems to me, to take *some* action, when we see that someone is in desperate need of help. However, it is very objectionable indeed to have a system, reminiscent of Strindberg's play, *The Father*, where the next of kin take an active part in the decision to commit someone (and where, for example, your spouse might come to lure you into the straitjacket). This decision should be taken by the administrative court and by the administrative court alone. As we have seen, not even doctors should take part in the decision, let alone the next of kin.

The main reason for not allowing the next of kin to take part in the decision is the fact that, even if they know the patient well, they are not versed in the kind of decision-making to be undertaken by the administrative court. And the patient is entitled to a *competent* handling of his or her case. This is part and parcel of the ideal of judicial security.

Another reason for not allowing the next of kin to take part in the decision is, of course, that the interests of the next of kin may be *at variance* with the interests of the person to be compulsorily admitted.

Finally, even if this is not the case, the person to be committed may *suspect* it to be the case. And this very suspicion may be detrimental to the social network of the patient.

We must bear in mind that the kind of patient we are discussing here may well suffer from delusions and be at risk of developing paranoid delusions in general and, in particular, paranoid delusions about the next of kin. Society should not contribute to this very sad kind of development.

Coercive medication?

It is one thing to say that people who need psychiatric care, who are not capable of reaching an autonomous decision about the care and who refuse to accept the care needed, should be compulsorily committed to a closed ward in a psychiatric hospital, and quite a different thing to say that any kind of medication can be administered to them while they are detained. So the question needs to be addressed: what kind of medication *should* be given to them?

In the first place, these people should be protected against themselves. They should be stopped from committing suicide, or from otherwise hurting themselves, while in the grips of their psychosis. To the extent that medication is needed to this effect, it must be administered. This is not controversial.

Second, these people should be treated, not only in order to keep them alive, but with whatever medication is considered necessary to restore a capacity to make autonomous decisions. This too should not be very controversial.

Note that all this is well in line with how medication is given for somatic symptoms, in emergency situations, when no consent can be obtained from the patient. And it is in line with the Convention:

> When because of an emergency situation the appropriate consent cannot be obtained, any medically necessary intervention may be carried out immediately for the benefit of the health of the individual concerned.
>
> (Article 8)

However, no *other* kind of medication should be coercively or manipulatively given for mental illness.

The reason for this restricted use of compulsory medication for mental illness should be obvious. Once the patient is capable of making an autonomous decision, it is up the patient, not the care-giver, to decide what kind of medication should be administered.

This is how treatment for somatic disease is given. The patient is granted an absolute right to a veto against medication. There is no reason to treat medication for mental illness differently.

As a matter of fact, there are special reasons to treat medication for mental illness more, rather than less, restrictively. This is to do with the fact that medication for mental illness is much more controversial than medication for somatic problems. Medication for mental illness has been questioned on two main counts.

On the one hand, it has been questioned on grounds of efficiency. The causes behind mental illness are not very well known. Consequently, it is a moot question to what extent medication cures mental diseases, or even renders symptoms of mental illness less serious.

On the other hand, medication for mental illness has been questioned on the (moral) ground that it may be only too effective, in that it changes the personality of the person suffering from the illness. If this kind of medication, which changes the personality of the patient, is undertaken coercively, it may mean a serious assault on the patient.

I do not mean to say that, upon closer examination, either of these arguments will stand up. However, the mere possibility that they might be sound and, in fact, the very suspicion that this might be the case, is a good enough reason not to coercively (and unnecessarily) medicate patients suffering from mental illness.

The decision to use whatever medicine that, according to the doctor, might be indicated, should be placed in the hands of the patient, once he or she is capable of making an autonomous decision. Mental illness should be treated no differently in this respect from somatic disease.

As a matter of fact, when a patient has been coercively committed, there exists a special risk that the care-giver must carefully watch out for. The risk is that the patient who has been committed against his or her will gives up his or her own judgement once detained. He or she may come to agree to a treatment he or she would not have agreed to, had he or she dared, or found it worthwhile, to voice an opinion.

This means that no medication other than the ones indicated by the interest of protecting the life and health of the patient and of making him or her capable of exercising an autonomous will should be administered, with or without the consent of the compulsorily committed patient.

Does this mean that certain kinds of medication or treatment (such as ECT) should be explicitly forbidden? Does it mean that special rules should apply to clinical trials where compulsorily admitted patients are involved?

I think not. The crucial question here is whether these kinds of treatment and medication are acceptable at all. So if valid criticism can be put forward against their use, this should be a reason for not using them in psychiatric treatment in general, and not just in the particular cases where the treatment takes a coercive form.

It is in this perspective that medical authorities should assess anti-medical criticisms put forward for example by Thomas McKeown (1988). If certain therapies are considered generally acceptable, in spite of the fact that they have been subjected to criticism, they can be given to people who are compulsorily committed as well, it seems to me. They should be given to compulsorily committed persons when it is reasonable to presume that this is what these patients would have opted for themselves, had they been capable of reaching an autonomous decision. Their right to use of controversial therapies should not be restricted in any special way.

Note, however, that if a psychotic person has declared, in a living will, when he or she was not psychotic, that he or she does not want under any circumstances to have a certain kind of treatment, such as ECT or a particular drug, then this wish of the patient should be honoured even when he or she is psychotic.

This way of handling controversial therapies should provide an incentive to the medical and scientific community to try and find out whether these therapies really are efficient, and whether there really are no better options available or capable of being developed.

While participation in clinical trials *may* be acceptable, being in the best interests of the patients who are coercively detained, no *experimentation* involving any risk at all, no matter how small, but no benefit, should be allowed to take place with these patients, not even with their 'consent'.

In this I find the Convention too liberal. According to Article 17 of the Convention, under exceptional circumstances, research with no potential to produce results of direct benefit to the health of a person concerned, not competent to decide for him- or herself, may be conducted. It may be conducted if the person in question does not object, and if certain other provisions are met, the most important one being the following:

> [that] the research has the aim of contributing, through significant improvement in the scientific understanding of the individual's condition, disease or disorder, to the ultimate attainment of results capable of conferring benefit to the person concerned or to other persons in the same age category or afflicted with the same disease or disorder or having the same condition.
>
> (Article 17)

The reason for thinking this too liberal, and for wanting an absolute restriction in this field, is simple: the consent of these people, even if it can be gained, cannot be a true expression of their autonomous will.

Note that there is no solid ground for presumed consent in this area. For it is one thing to presume that a certain individual would have accepted the best possible treatment, if he or she had been capable of considering the problem rationally, and quite a different thing to presume that a certain individual would have volunteered for an experiment, for the sake of science or the wellbeing of other persons, if he or she had been capable of considering the offer rationally. We can have good reasons for the former presumption (when ill, people in general want to be cured), but never for the latter presumption (people typically *differ* with respect to their degree of willingness to make sacrifices for the sake of others).

Conclusion

When people who suffer from mental illness become incapable, because of their illness, of reaching a decision about their need for treatment, when they need treatment for their own sake (unless they are treated their health is put in jeopardy), then these people ought to be coercively admitted to a psychiatric ward and treated for their mental illness. This is in accordance with what I have called the Incompetency Model.

Moreover, all sorts of medication needed to safeguard their health should be given to these people, provided they have not, while capable of reaching an autonomous decision, declared that they do not wish to accept certain kinds of treatment.

Once they have reached a stage where they can make an autonomous decision, even if still mentally ill, they should be granted the right to a veto against treatment, just as all other people are, in relation to somatic health care. Mental illness is no different in this respect. If they want to leave the psychiatric ward they should be allowed to do so. If they remain in the ward, they should still have a right to a veto against certain kinds of treatment.

The decision compulsorily to admit a patient who is mentally ill to a closed psychiatric ward should be taken by a court of law. No doctor should take part in the decision. Neither should the next of kin of the patient. Neither the doctor nor the next of kin has the required expertise.

However, a doctor must provide evidence about the mental status of the patient to the court. This should not be the doctor who treats the patient, however, but an independent witness. The patient must know that he or she can trust 'his' or 'her' doctor. And the patient should be granted a competent attorney.

Finally, the sole purpose for which a person may be legitimately compulsorily admitted is his or her *own* need for treatment, not the needs of any other person or the needs of 'society'.

This is acknowledged in the Convention, but not in existing laws in most European countries. The reason why it is not acknowledged in actual law is to do both with prejudices in relation to mental illness and with the manner in which people who commit crimes under influence of mental illness are taken care of in these countries. Since these people cannot, according to the prevailing ideology, be put in prison, they must be subjected to civil commitment. Thus we have a sinister mixture of care and punishment.

Here we need a total reform of the entire attitude to mental illness. A sharp demarcation line must be drawn between care and punishment.

In this chapter I have indicated how this can be accomplished in relation to civil commitment. In the next chapter I conclude my description of the reformed system I want to defend, by specifying its implications for forensic psychiatric care.

6

FORENSIC PSYCHIATRY

Sometimes people commit crimes influenced by mental illness. In principle, there seem to be three main ways in which society can react to these people. I will refer to these ways as 'the Excuse Model', 'the Mixed Model' and 'the Full Responsibility Model' respectively.

These three models could be described as follows.

1   *The Excuse Model* We excuse people who commit crimes influenced by mental illness and consider them unfit for trial. If they are dangerous, they are detained in the interest of the safety of other citizens. But this decision to detain them is taken independently of any judicial assessment of the crime they have committed and it is not founded upon any statute of criminal law. Treatment may be enforced, but if it is enforced, it is enforced because of their mental illness, not because of the crime they have committed. If necessary, they are incapacitated, but they are not punished. As far as I know this is the model in use in all European countries except Sweden and a few North American States.

2   *The Mixed Model* We hold people who commit crimes influenced by mental illness responsible for their criminal offence, we convict them in accordance with criminal law, but we do not sentence them to gaol. Instead we sentence them to psychiatric treatment. So, in a way, the psychiatric treatment they receive is the form their punishment actually takes. This model is practised in Sweden. It is also practised in a few North American States.

3   *The Full Responsibility Model* We apply criminal justice to people who commit crimes influenced by mental illness and sentence them to gaol (or whatever kind of punishment may be in order for the crime in question);[1] however, if this is what they need, we offer them (voluntary)

---

1 In the present context I will take it for granted that imprisonment is the standard form of punishment. This is not to say that, in many cases, other kinds of punishment may not prove superior. In particular, it might seem a good idea to oblige people who have committed crimes to compensate their victims, or make some kind of reparation.

psychiatric treatment. If they are not capable of reaching an autonomous decision about their own psychiatric needs, but need treatment, we enforce this treatment upon them (in their own interests). However, this decision to treat them against their will is not taken in accordance with criminal law. The rationale for the enforced treatment is their need and their inability to acknowledge their own best interests. The compulsion ends as soon as they are capable of deciding for themselves whether to go on with the treatment (if it is still needed) or not (and return to gaol).

The advantages of the Full Responsibility Model are fairly obvious. First, if we adopt it, we get a clear delineation of roles, which engenders a more professional treatment. We allow the psychiatrist to be just a doctor, not a warden. We allow that punishment is one thing and treatment another.

Second, on the Full Responsibility Model, with a small exception to be noted below, we liberate psychiatry from the duty of deciding whether people are fit to stand trial; we liberate psychiatrists from the task of deciding if people who were mentally ill when they committed criminal offences 'could have acted otherwise' – a hopeless task (the philosopher knows).

Third, on the Full Responsibility Model we allow psychiatrists to live up to their professional ethical code (the Declaration of Hawaii), and to the Convention (requiring, we remember, that no one be coercively treated unless 'without such treatment, serious harm is likely to result to his or her health'), which they cannot do if they agree to detain those who are 'dangerously insane'.

On both the Excuse Model and the Mixed Model psychiatrists have to flout their professional code (the Declaration of Hawaii) and the Convention. They act against the Declaration of Hawaii and the Convention when (on the Excuse Model) they detain people, not because this is what these people themselves need but because, after having been considered unfit to stand trial, these people are considered dangerous to others. James C. Beck has made the following comment about this, relating to US practice:

> Incompetent defendants who do not meet civil commitment standards are to be released from hospital. However, judges are reluctant to release incompetent patients charged with serious violent crimes. Often, judges will find that these patients meet standards for commitment on evidence which would not be sufficient for commitment of other persons.
>
> (1996: 17)

And they act against the Declaration of Hawaii again when (on the Mixed Model) they feel that there is no more treatment they can offer a person who has been sentenced to psychiatric treatment, but where an administrative court rejects their claim that their patient should be set free. In the circumstances, the person is detained in a psychiatric clinic without being offered any treatment whatever. The rationale behind this rejection on the part of the court of law, of course, is not medical. The rationale is that these people are still considered dangerous to others. But to abide by such a ruling by the court of law is inconsistent with what is stated in the Declaration of Hawaii:

> If a patient or some third party demands actions contrary to scientific knowledge or ethical principles the psychiatrist must refuse to cooperate.

> (Article 7)

Fourth, on the Full Responsibility Model, by allowing psychiatrists to abide by the Declaration of Hawaii, we improve their bad reputation. By giving them a strictly medical role, outside the repressive system of punishment, we make it possible for their patients to have faith in them, in a way in which the patients cannot have faith in their psychiatrists when they are part and parcel of the repressive system.

Finally, on the Full Responsibility Model we treat psychically ill persons as 'normal', we allow them to repent their crimes, which assists their recovery. This is a way of counteracting all sorts of prejudice against those who are mentally ill. This also renders easier their return to society, after having served their time. For, in particular, if they are quickly cured and released (because they have been quickly cured) after having committed horrible crimes, it is more than likely that people in general will look askance at them. If, instead, they have both been cured and served some time for their crimes, people will find it easier to forgive them for what they have done.

However, strong objections to the Full Responsibility Model immediately come to mind. Some of them concern details, others are of a principled nature. Let me start with those concerning details.

Minor objections First, is it not absurd to convict a mentally ill person for murder, it might be asked. The mentally ill person did not know what he was doing, it might be thought. In order to punish a person we must prove the existence of *mens rea* (a guilty mind). This is what criminal law in most societies and in most cases requires. But a mentally ill person does not act on purpose, he does not intend his actions, he does not know what he is doing, nor does he know that what he is doing is wrong, so *mens rea* cannot be proved.

I concede that there may be cases where a mentally ill person does not know what he does. Take for example a person who squeezes the head of a child in the belief that it is a lemon. Or, take a mentally impaired person like Lennie in *Of Mice and Men*. When killing persons he is not even aware of what he is doing, or at least he is not aware of it until it is too late.

These persons should not (and cannot) be convicted according to criminal justice, I concede, so even on the Full Responsibility Model there is *some* role for psychiatrists to play in court. Psychiatric expertise must ascertain whether a person who has seemingly committed a crime really did know what he was doing.

However, the cases where the criminal offender does not know what he is doing are extremely rare.[2] It is much more common that mentally ill persons who harm other persons know perfectly well what they are doing. They may feel that they have good reason to do what they do (they have been instructed to do it by strange 'forces', for example), but this does not mean that they do not act on purpose. And they know that what they are doing is illegal. So there is no theoretical obstacle to my proposal concerning these people. It is possible to prove *mens rea* and it is possible, if we decide to do so, to hold them responsible for their criminal acts. If this is how we want to proceed, we can treat these people as 'normal'.

Second, it might be argued, is it not a hopeless task to treat these people for their psychiatric disorders in prison? In order to treat them properly, don't we need the resources of a mental hospital?

Of course we do. But then they should be taken out of prison and into an 'ordinary' mental hospital for treatment. This is no different from how we proceed when a prisoner needs surgery. We then take him out of prison to a hospital, where he receives the treatment he needs. When he is fit for it, we send him back to prison. The same procedure should be followed when the needed treatment is psychiatric. Once again, the normalisation of psychiatric illness that goes with my proposal is here an advantage.

Principled objections   Let me now turn to the principled objections to the Full Responsibility Model. Three objections in particular come to mind.

First, is it not *unfair* to sentence people who could not help doing what they did to gaol, it might be asked.

Second, setting the question of fairness to one side, is it not *inhumane* to sentence mentally ill persons to gaol? Is it not inhumane to the mentally ill persons themselves and does it not mean that they will be a burden to other prisoners?

Finally, would it not be hazardous to set insane people free from prison (because they have served their time), when they are still considered dangerous? Would this not be to put into *jeopardy* the life and safety of their potential victims?

---

2 I have no statistical evidence to rely on here, but I have questioned several experts in the field who claim that, at most, only a small percentage of those who are considered unfit for trial fall into this category.

Let me discuss these objections in order.

The argument from retributive justice

Is it unfair to sentence people who could not help doing what they did to gaol?

The answer to this question is less straightforward than it might at first appear. Let me take as the point of departure of my argument the most well-known and most extensively discussed example, the McNaghten case. Daniel McNaghten, suffering from the paranoid delusion that the Prime Minister, Sir Robert Peel, was part of the plot to persecute and to destroy him, shot at and killed Peel's secretary believing him to be Peel. According to the McNaghten Rules of 1843, in order to establish a defence of insanity it must be proved that the accused 'was labouring under such a defect of reason, from disease of the mind, as not to know the nature and quality of the act he was doing; or, if he did know it, that he did not know he was doing what was wrong'.

Would it not have been unfair to punish McNaghten, it might be asked. For, surely, he did not know what he was doing or, at least, he did not know that it was wrong.

The point is not simply that he mistook the secretary for the Prime Minister nor that he wrongly believed that he acted out of self-defence. The point must rather be that his belief that the Prime Minister threatened him, and that he had to shoot him in self-defence, was compulsive. It was, as such, a symptom of his mental illness. And because of its compulsive nature his very act was compulsive. He could not help doing what he did. But it is not fair to punish a person for something he could not help doing.

It is far from clear, it seems to me, that McNaghten could not help doing what he did. In order to ascertain whether he could or could not help doing what he did, we must decide what this means. There is a sense of the phrase 'could not help doing what he did' in which no one could ever help doing what he does. Is this relevant in the present context? And there are senses of this phrase in which McNaghten did probably know what he did and could have helped doing it. Are they relevant?

But this is beside the point of my argument. For I am prepared to question, not only the argument as such, but also the foundation on which it is based. When we say that it is unfair to punish a person for something he cannot help doing, we want to make a distinction. We tacitly assume that it *is* fair to punish a person for a criminal offence that he *can* help performing, i.e. we presuppose a theory of retributive justice according to which a person can deserve (morally) to be punished. I would have none of this. I cannot go very deeply into this problem. Let me just make some brief comments.

When we say that it is unfair to punish a person for a criminal offence he could not help committing, we presuppose something like the following. We accept the idea put forward by Immanuel Kant to the following effect:

> Even if a civil society were to dissolve itself by common agreement of all its members . . . the last murderer remaining in prison must first be executed, so that everyone will duly receive what his actions are worth and so that the bloodguilt thereof will not be fixed on the people because they failed to insist on carrying out the punishment; for if they fail to do so, they may be regarded as accomplices in this public violation of legal justice.
>
> ('The Right to Punish', in Murphy 1973: 37)

Or, at least we take as our point of departure some idea put forward by G.E. Moore, that:

> The infliction of pain on a person whose state of mind is bad may, if the pain be not too intense, create a state of things that is better *on the whole*. It is in this way that the theory of vindictive punishment may be vindicated. The infliction of pain on a person whose state of mind is bad may, if the pain be not too intense, create a state of things that is better *on the whole* than if the evil state of mind had existed unpunished. Whether such a state of things can ever constitute a *positive* good, is another question.
>
> (1903: 214)

I consider all this as superstition.

Contra Kant I want to object as follows: Kant seems to think that society has a positive obligation to punish the criminal, irrespective of whether there are any good 'side-effects' of the punishment. How can he think so? Does he believe that the punishment annuls the crime? But could this be right? To be sure, the punishment does not annul the *harm* done by the criminal. But perhaps it does annul the *guilt* of the offender? If it does, it might perhaps be argued that the punishment is something society owes to *the criminal*.

Now, *does* the punishment annul the guilt of the offender? Well, I must confess that I do not believe there is any such thing as guilt, so I believe there is nothing for the punishment to annul. However, even if there is such a thing as guilt, it seems indeed more appropriate to say that the criminal *himself* should get rid of his guilt, rather than society. The criminal could, for example, say he is sorry, he could actually be sorry for what he has done, and try to compensate the victims of his crime, and so forth.

As a matter of fact, if the punishment annuls the guilt, it must be *because* it makes the victim himself take responsibility for what he has done. However, it is far from certain that the punishment will have this effect. And, even more important in the present, retributive context, it seems quite appropriate to say that it is really not a matter for *society* to rid the criminal of his guilt.

We, the society, are not to blame for what he has done. If the guilt of the criminal can be taken away at all, it is something that should be done by the criminal himself. After all, according to retributivism, he, and he alone, is responsible for what he has done.

Against this it might be argued that, even if (according to retributivism) society has no obligation to punish criminals who are guilty, society is, at least, forbidden to punish criminals who are without guilt (who could not help doing what they did). There is something to this objection, but it is not decisive.

For if society punishes a person who is not guilty for the crime he has committed (if, as a matter of fact, he could not help committing it), and if it punishes him in the belief that he is guilty (in the false belief that he *could* help committing the crime and that, for this reason, he has to be punished), society makes a mistake. However, if society punishes him, not for retributivist reasons, but for *preventive* reasons, then I cannot see why this would be objectionable on a retributivist count. What society is doing is not 'punishing', in the retributivist sense of the word, at all! And, of course, this kind of reaction – we may call it 'punishment' or something else - is what I think society should take up, with respect both to criminals who act out of mental illness and to criminals whose crimes can be explained in some other manner (for example, with reference to their childhood, their genome or their social situation).

The rationale for the punishment (or the social reaction) in particular cases should be that the criminals had committed the crime for which they were convicted (irrespective of whether they could help doing what they did). But the rationale for the *institution* of punishment, and the actual *form* it takes, should be utilitarian (preventive of crime).

Contra Moore's ideal utilitarianism I'm tempted simply to say: how can two wrongs make a right? And even if, somehow, they can, the value of the organic whole consisting of a criminal suffering and this being in accordance with justice, is very *speculative*. On the other hand, the suffering of the criminal is *certainly* something bad. And I do not think it wise for society to cause certain harms in order to obtain merely very speculative goods.

If justice is of value in itself, in the way indicated by Moore, it seems to be a value which is like objective aesthetic values, if such values exist. And while it would be all right for an individual to make sacrifices on his own, in order to create, say, beauty, it would not be in order to make other people suffer in order to obtain aesthetic value. So it was not only wrong, it was *very* wrong, when the Roman emperor Heliogabalus had people decapitated on grass, simply because he enjoyed the look of red on green. Even if this was beautiful, and even if beauty were a value, it was very wrong to do so.

Of course, this rejection of retributivism is not something I can fully substantiate in the present context. However, my rejection of it is not very spectacular. And it should be noted that, if I am correct in it, then we could very well go on saying that it is unfair to punish a person who committed a crime and could not help doing so, but we should *also* say, equally, that it is unfair to punish a person who committed a crime and *could* help doing so. In both cases we use these persons as means to a certain end. We punish them in order to reduce crime rates.

Of course, there is another sense, in which neither of them is treated unfairly. The treatment of them is fair if it is necessary to take these measures against these people in order to reduce crime rates and if these measures are not in any way unusual or cruel, or do not flout the ideal of judicial security.

The proper objective of punishment, then, in my opinion, is prevention. No one 'deserves' his punishment in any deeper sense than this: he committed the crime for which he was tried, and the consequences of punishing people in his situation are, on the whole, good.

Now it might be tempting to object, however, that while punishment of sane people may deter from crime, punishment of insane people does not deter. People who commit crime, influenced by mental illness, do not calculate, they do not pay any respect to the risk that they will be punished. Therefore, it cannot be part of an optimal system of sanctions that we punish mentally ill persons.

We should resist this line of argument. In the first place, it is not very far-fetched to believe that even mentally ill persons may take some kind of precaution and show *some* kind of prudence. Moreover, they may have some idea of what is right and wrong. They too should be set straight! The fact that the action they contemplate is prohibited by law may lead them to suspect that it might be morally wrong, after all. And this belief may have some restraining effect on them.

Second, and even more important, the fact that we punish insane people may deter *sane* people from committing crimes in the hope that they will get away with what they are doing, in particular by pleading insanity.

The crucial factor here is not whether it is easy or difficult to fool psychiatric experts. Perhaps it is difficult. However, even if, as a matter of fact, it is difficult, some people may (falsely) come to *believe* that it is easy. These people are deterred when they realise that *no one* can get away with their crime by pleading insanity.

Certainly, there is a price to be paid in terms of judicial security for the system I advocate. If the Full Responsibility Model were to be adopted, each of us must fear that, if we became mentally ill and committed crimes under influence of our mental disorder, we might have to suffer the consequences. On the other hand, existing models have their price as well. Each of us must fear that some people may contemplate serious crimes in the hope that they will get away with them by pleading insanity.

The latter price seems to me to be the higher one to pay, in particular, if what is said in the next section in defence against the objection on grounds of humaneness is taken into account.

The argument from humaneness

Setting aside the question of (retributive) justice, is it not still *inhumane* to sentence mentally ill persons to gaol? Is it not inhumane treatment of the mentally ill persons themselves, and does it not mean that they will become a burden to other prisoners?

There is much force in this objection, if we take as our point of departure actual prisons in most actual countries of the world. However, the reason that it would be inhumane to sentence mentally ill persons to gaol is that most prisons are, generally speaking, inhumane. The proper reaction to this, it seems to me, is not to spare mentally ill persons from going to gaol but to make our prisons places where *no one* is treated badly (other than by being coercively committed and hence deprived of liberty, of course), whether they are sane or insane. No one should be treated *merely* as a means.

This is a question of economic resources, of course, but at least in the rich parts of the world such as the European countries, the US, Canada, Japan and Australia, there should be no problem in raising necessary funds. The pay-off in the long run must be good.

Obviously, most people who go to gaol do so, primarily, because they have committed a criminal offence and have been convicted for it, but more basically because of some kind of failure in their lives. They are often ill-educated and poorly socialised, or they have genetic disorders and personality traits that make them ill-suited to social life. They should all of them be treated humanely. There is much to be gained from this, it seems to me. There is much to be gained in humanitarian terms, of course, but also in terms of efficiency. If we treat them well, if we take as our point of departure their individual needs, there is a chance that we will be able to help them to a well-ordered life.

Does this mean that we should not punish them? I think not. We need a system of punishment in order to deter, not only or primarily criminals, but ourselves from committing certain actions. But the deterrent effect is not simply dependent on the harsh treatment of prisoners. The crucial point is that there be *some* reaction from society, when we commit criminal offences, and that the reaction be firm and immediate. This is compatible, however, with the reaction being humane.

Most people would like to stay out of prison, even if prisoners are offered possibilities of education, medical care and, when necessary, psychiatric treatment. After all, in a humane society, all these things are available to people outside prison as well as to prisoners. So the differences between the former and the latter categories are important enough to motivate people who are prepared to calculate and be prudent to attempt to stay outside prison.

When, in spite of this, some people end up in prison, this is a signal that something has gone wrong in their lives. They call for our help. We should not hesitate to offer it.

The argument from jeopardy

Setting aside the problems with fairness and humaneness, would it still not be hazardous to set people free, just because they have served their time, when they could still be considered dangerous to others (because of mental illness)? Would this not be to put into jeopardy the life and safety of their potential victims?

I admit that there is some force in the argument. Of course, if we accept the Full Responsibility Model we need to take some precautions here. We cannot just set free people who have committed serious crimes after only a short time in gaol, if they are still considered dangerous because of their mental illness (but cannot be treated for the illness because they refuse to accept treatment). It should be noted, however, that if they are dangerous to themselves, and incapable of reaching an autonomous decision as to their own medical needs, we *can* enforce psychiatric treatment upon them, without violating the Declaration of Hawaii.

Still this may not seem to be adequate as an answer to the objection from jeopardy. What can we add to the answer? I suggest the following. When people commit very serious crimes, when they kill or harm other people, they should be sentenced to a very long time in prison.

I see nothing objectionable in this. After all, they have committed very serious crimes. Then it is only natural that the reaction from society be strong. However, if they repent, and behave in a manner that allows us to predict that they will not commit crimes again, then they should be set free on parole, and, if everything works out well, they can be absolved from their punishment.

All sorts of leniency provision should be tried. A similar possibility should be open for those criminals who are mentally ill. If they accept treatment for their mental illness, and if they recover from it, then they too should be set free on parole. And, if things work out well, they can be absolved from their punishments.

Against this suggestion it might be tempting to object that, if such a system is practised then, after all, predictions of dangerousness *will* be the basis for decisions about whether to detain a person or not. And have I not repeatedly argued that this must come to flout the ideal of judicial security?

There is a crucial difference, however, between, on the one hand, detaining a person, in the first place, because he or she might turn out to become dangerous to other persons, and, on the other hand, releasing, on predictive grounds, a person who has on other (punitive) grounds been previously detained.

When people commit crimes they know that this is how they may come to be treated. If they do not like being treated in this manner, then they should abstain from committing crimes.

As a matter of fact, in this field I think there is *much* room for assessments of dangerousness. In the circumstances, such assessments can be performed without the ideal of judicial security being flouted. They can be performed on all persons who are in gaol, not only on those who are mentally ill, but on other prisoners as well.

It would be preferable, of course, if certain objective criteria could be established in this field. I think of criteria such as, for example, that for a person with a certain personality type, it is crucial (to the prediction of dangerousness) whether he or she undergoes a certain therapy or not. For persons with a different personality type, or a different diagnosis, the crucial thing (to the prediction of dangerousness) may be instead whether he or she gives up the abuse of drugs, or accepts a job that is offered.

On such grounds people may well be released from prison, or kept in prison, even if the predictive instruments are less than perfect. And, of course, such predictive instruments will always remain less than perfect. Here society can opt for a generally agreed upon, and politically established, degree of risk acceptance.[3] And here there is room for scientific development of better predictive techniques.

A special category, existing somewhere in a continuum from mentally healthy to mentally ill persons, are those who sexually abuse other people (paedophiles, for example). They should of course be offered a similar choice. If they accept treatment (even such treatment as medical castration) and if they accept some kind of control to ensure that they continue their treatment, and if it can be established that such measures tend to make them become (sufficiently) less dangerous to others, then they could be set free.

It is a moot question whether these people are mentally ill or not. On the Full Responsibility Model, we need not go into this complicated discussion. I see this as an advantage. We treat them as normal, we punish them for their deeds, but we offer them whatever treatment exists for their problem.

---

3 I owe this observation to the Swedish forensic psychiatrist Sten Levander.

Even if the punishment they undergo is severe, there is a possibility for them to escape from it; by accepting, and voluntarily undergoing, successful treatment.

Conclusion

The main thrust of the argument of this chapter is as follows. Rather than considering people who commit crimes under influence of mental illness unfit for trial (in accordance with the Excuse Model), we ought to try them in court (in accordance with the Full Responsibility Model). If it can be proved that they have committed the crime they are tried for, and provided they knew what they were doing (even if, perversely, because of mental illness, they believed that they only did what they had to do), we ought to sentence them to gaol rather than to psychiatric treatment (the Mixed Model).

This does not mean that we should treat them badly or *merely* as a means to an end (deterrence). On the contrary, mentally ill prisoners, like other prisoners, have a right to have their basic needs satisfied. Those who need psychiatric treatment should be offered psychiatric treatment, those who need social training should be offered social training, those who need treatment for a somatic problem should receive such treatment, and so forth.

The advantages of the Full Responsibility Model are obvious. If we implement it, then we make a sharp division between health care and punishment, we improve the reputation of psychiatric care, we allow psychiatrists to abide by the Declaration of Hawaii, we treat mentally ill persons as 'normal', thereby counteracting various kinds of prejudice against them, and we allow them to repent of their crimes and to learn, to the extent that it is possible for them to do so, about right and wrong conduct.

If we reject as outmoded and false the idea that some people (morally) deserve to be punished (irrespective of the consequences of punishing them), then there is no problem in terms of retributive justice with the model I advocate.

There are practical problems with it, however, but these can be handled. We can handle them if we do not hesitate to allocate economic resources necessary to ascertain a just, humane and finely tuned system of punishment, meeting the needs of each individual undergoing punishment.

7

FOETAL/MATERNAL CONFLICTS

Advances in medicine have prepared the grounds for a new kind of possible conflict, to wit, a conflict between pregnant women and their foetuses.

Of course, there exists an old and well-known *aspect* of this kind of conflict, the problem of abortion. Can a woman, by not carrying her pregnancy to term, harm the interests of her foetus? But added to this familiar problem are a vast number of new ones.

New knowledge about the impact of the lifestyle chosen by the pregnant woman on the health and safety of the foetus gives rise to the question: must the pregnant woman take the health of the foetus into consideration, when she chooses how to live?

New medical advances may even present a pregnant woman with the option to take medication, and even to undergo surgery, in the best interests of her foetus.

There are even some rare cases where surgery on the foetus during pregnancy may be indicated. Does this mean that the pregnant woman has an obligation to take such medication or surgery, or allow the foetus she carries to be operated on, in the best interests, not of herself, but of the foetus?

In the present chapter I will discuss these problems. I focus, not on the individual moral question, but on the legal aspect.

I think it *obvious* that a pregnant woman may have *some* moral responsibility with respect to her foetus (and the future child and human being the foetus will develop into, if carried to term); however, this does not necessarily mean that society has a right (or obligation) to coerce her into doing her moral duty with respect to the foetus/future child. I will discuss to what extent society has such a right/obligation.

I will start my discussion with a brief note about the traditional aspect of the problem, i.e. on the question of abortion. I then move on to discuss the more spectacular, new aspects of the problem of foetal/maternal conflicts, concerning new medical information and new medical techniques.

Abortion

I do not intend to settle the question of the morality of abortion. This problem is way beyond the scope of the present study.[1] It must suffice here to note that, according to most thinkers, some abortions are morally wrong while others are morally permitted. This is my opinion too. In particular, I believe that, to the extent that a couple (or a single woman) can make the world better by having the child, they ought to have it. If the world becomes worse if they have it, they should choose abortion. On this – utilitarian – view, abortion is not special. It can be wrong to have an abortion, but it can be wrong too, equally wrong, as it were, not to conceive a child.

This utilitarian view is only one among many possible ideas about the morality of abortion, of course. Most thinkers would agree, I suppose, that there is something to the utilitarian consideration. However, they would like to add to it.

Some would like to add that the foetus has a *right* to life, irrespective of how the sum total of wellbeing in the universe would be affected by the pregnancy being carried to term. But most who argue along these lines would like to add that, if the pregnancy is not a voluntary undertaking by the woman, such as when the foetus is the result of rape, the right of the pregnant woman to get rid of the pregnancy overrides the right to life, on the part of the foetus.

Still others would add that, to the extent that the life awaiting the child would be a miserable one, its right to life is overridden, or simply absent.

Others again would argue that it is morally forbidden to end innocent human lives, period. This means that most abortions are wrong. However, some who believe in the obligation not to kill would be willing to make an exception when it comes to a foetus resulting from rape (considering abortion in analogy with self-defence), or when it comes to a foetus that will result in a child with a miserable life waiting for it (considering abortion in analogy with mercy killing). And, with reference to the doctrine of double effect, they may want to argue that an operation that saves the life of the pregnant woman is warranted or even obligatory, even if it must lead (as a foreseen but not sought for consequence of the operation) to the death of the foetus she is carrying.

Which one among all these competing views is the correct one?

This is indeed a difficult matter to settle. People who have devoted their entire intellectual lives to the question disagree. But then it would be rash for society to adopt any view in particular, as the correct or appropriate one.

1 The best review of this discussion, I am afraid, is in Swedish. I refer to Christian Munthe's book *Livets slut i livets början* (1992).

As a matter of fact, the complexity and difficulty of the moral question is a very good reason for a free right to abortion. When society as such, when political authorities, cannot reach a decision acceptable to all or even to a majority (there may well exist cyclical majorities in this field), it should give up the ambition to reach any decision at all. It is better to have individual couples, and, in the final analysis, when the fathers are absent or the parents disagree, individual women, taking the decisions.

Another reason for allowing women to make the decision for or against abortion is that, according to most views about the morality of abortion, there exist *some* considerations that may tip the argumentative balance in favour of abortion. And the pregnant women themselves are experts on these considerations.

I think here of such facts as whether the foetus is or is not a result of rape, or facts about the kind of life awaiting the possible child. While there are no generally recognised experts on the abstract moral question about abortion, there *are* experts on these empirical and, according to most moral theories, morally *relevant* facts: the pregnant women themselves.

The pregnant woman knows better than anyone else about whether the foetus she carries is or is not the result of rape, and also, if properly aided and advised by doctors, social workers, and others, about the kind of life she can offer her possible child.

Finally, we know from the discussion in Chapter 3 that, for reasons to do with the Nazi Spectre, there exists a strong presumption in favour of not allowing political authorities to meddle with our reproductive decisions. This presumption goes in favour of having a free right to abortion too, placing the hard decision about carrying, or not carrying, the pregnancy to term firmly in the hands of the pregnant woman.

But surely this reasoning must be mistaken, it might be objected. It is true indeed that competent thinkers disagree about the morality of abortion, but so do they about the morality of killing, in general. And, to be sure, we cannot leave it up to the prospective murderer to decide whether to murder or not. It would follow that it cannot be up to the pregnant woman to decide whether to carry her pregnancy to term or not.

There is a crucial difference between the two cases, however. It is true that in neither of them does there exist any unanimous expert moral opinion. However, with respect to murder (the individual killing of inno-cent – born – people against their will), there exists a consideration that is not at all controversial. Unless we prohibit murder, and punish those who violate the prohibition, we will all come to feel very insecure. It is in the interest of us all to have murder prohibited (and severely punished). *This* is why the decision to murder or not to murder cannot be placed in the hands of the prospective murderer.

There exists no similar argument to the effect that the decisions about abortion cannot be placed in the hands of pregnant women. When many women chose to have abortions, even in cases where many people would find that they are doing something wrong, the wrong they do is not felt as a *threat* to anyone else.[2]

We who are grown up and contemplate the matter cannot be aborted (any longer), so we have nothing to fear personally from the right to free abortion. And those who have something to fear personally from it, those who can still be aborted (the foetuses), do not contemplate the matter. On some understanding of the word, they are not even 'persons'. And be that as it may, being persons or not, the foetuses feel no fear for their own sake. They have no concern (yet) for their own future.

If this is accepted, that the pregnant woman should be allowed to make her own decision as to whether she should carry her pregnancy to term, then, it might be thought, there exists no problem in relation to other kinds of intervention. If the woman has a right to *kill* her foetus, then she cannot have an obligation to choose a certain lifestyle, or to undergo surgery, in the best interests of the foetus, it might be thought.

We should resist this line of argument. It is one thing to choose abortion and have no future child, and quite a different thing to choose not to have an abortion, and act in a manner that causes harm to the future child (and future person).

Even if women have, and ought to have, the former (legal) right, to wit, the right to abortion, it is an open question whether they should also have a legal right to harm their foetuses (in a way that means problems for the future children).

I now turn to this question.

A presumption for coercion

If a woman, because of mental illness or drug abuse, chooses a lifestyle detrimental to the interests of her future child, and if she is not capable of reaching an autonomous decision about her own need for treatment, it should be possible for society to see to it that she is coerced into receiving treatment. This is in line with the main thrust of the argument of this book. This treatment of the pregnant woman for her own sake may happen to be in the best interests of her future child. In fact, it often is. So there is some room for intervention against some women who put their future children's health at risk.

---

2 Selective abortions have indeed been considered a threat against living people with the handicap that motivated the abortion in question. And this is the best argument against allowing selective abortions. However, for reasons already discussed, this reason is not strong enough to warrant a total prohibition. And if some selective abortions are to be allowed, all had better be allowed. Otherwise the political authorities or the doctors would have to decide what kinds of handicap render a life not worthy of living. And this might pose a real threat to people living with these handicaps.

But what if her choice of lifestyle is not the result of mental illness or delirium? What if it is voluntarily undertaken? Or, what if the treatment needed by the foetus is not needed at all by the woman? Should society then be allowed to intervene using coercive measures?

There exists a strong presumption in favour of allowing society to coerce a woman into adopting a lifestyle favourable to the health of her future child, and even in favour of coercing women to take medication or undergo surgery in the interests of their future children.

If women are coerced into respecting the interests of their future children, then this coercion is not paternalistic. If it takes place, it takes place in the interest of a third party, the future child, and not in the interest of the pregnant woman.

And, from the point of view of the future child, very much may be at stake. The difference may be a difference between an ordinary, healthy life, and a life of poor quality with a severe handicap.

There is a problem in this context, however, which is to do with the ideal of judicial security. If coercion is accepted, the only acceptable *form* it could take would be through punishment. This should be clear from what has been argued in previous chapters, in particular the ones about forensic psychiatry and defence against infectious disease.

Political authorities could stipulate maternal duties and, to the extent that women do not abide by the rules, they could be prosecuted and convicted in a court of law. However, society should not (directly) coerce women into abiding by the rules. For this would be to flout the ideal of judicial security. Every person has a right to physical integrity.

Now, this use of criminal justice is a clumsy way of safeguarding the interests of future children. It is not only a clumsy way, but it is a way that may as such pose a threat to the interests of the child. The punishment may hurt the woman and so, indirectly, be at variance with the interests of the child. Furthermore, punishing the mother is a way of safeguarding the interests of future children that does not prevent harm in the individual case. The punishment is meted out when the harm has already come about. So if the system be effective at all, it must be effective because of its preventive effects.

Would it have such a preventive effect? And, if it would, are there no *better* ways of achieving the same preventive effect?

After these very general remarks, let us now consider the problem more in detail.

Lifestyle

The choice of lifestyle by the mother-to-be may affect (negatively) the health and wellbeing of the future child. In particular, the use of drugs and smoking may be detrimental to the child.

All this means that there are good reasons for the mother-to-be to abstain from drugs and smoking. This indicates also that there are good reasons for the health care system to encourage pregnant women to choose a lifestyle compatible with the interests of their future child. There is good reason to *educate* women, and to provide *help* and *services* for those among them who have difficulties in abiding by the rules that can be suggested to them. All this should be perfectly uncontroversial.

Moreover, sometimes coercive measures can be legitimately taken against women who, through their choice of lifestyle, put their future children at risk; these coercive measures are legitimate to the extent that they are taken, not with the direct intention of securing the health of the future child, but with the intention of securing the health of the pregnant woman. This kind of coercion is legitimate to the extent that those who are submitted to it really need it, and are incapable of making an autonomous decision with respect to it. This is true, of course, of a woman who is not only drug addicted, but suffers from delirium. And it is true of some women who suffer from mental illness.

However, what if the pregnant woman *is* capable of exercising an autonomous decision with respect to her lifestyle, but refuses to adapt it to the needs of the future child? Or, what if she is not *capable* of changing her lifestyle (she is addicted to the use of a certain drug, say), but does not *want* to give up her addiction (she is capable of deciding autonomously, we suppose, whether to accept a certain cure against her addiction)? Does all this mean that society should control her behaviour, in the best interest of her future child?

This is what has happened recently in the US, in Canada and Australia. In the US, both South Dakota and Wisconsin have adopted laws allowing compulsory admission of drug-addicted pregnant women, and several states seem to be following suit (Langton 1998).

A much publicised case in Winnipeg, Manitoba, Canada, eventually ended up before the Supreme Court of Canada (Makin 1997). The case began in August 1996 when a Winnipeg judge ordered a pregnant glue addict woman into the custody of social welfare authorities. The woman was said to sniff substances such as glue, paint thinner and nail-polish remover. She already had three children; all were wards of the state and two had neurological damage. A psychiatrist had found the woman herself mentally competent, so it had not been possible for the judge to apply the province's Mental Health Act to the case.

> 'It's not something that we did lightly,' said Elizabeth Sellick, the head of legal services for Winnipeg Child and Family Services, which brought the case forward. 'But I think almost all of the people who work with us will tell you that this is a very big problem.' . . . Ms. Sellick acknowledged that she too has concerns

about individual liberties, but questioned the right of the woman to continue abusing solvents while pregnant. 'Does she have the right to continue having damaged children?'

(*The Globe and Mail*, Toronto, 7 August 1996)

The child was born, apparently healthy, in December 1996.

Is this kind of reaction on the part of the society warranted?

We have already seen that a presumption for coercively controlling a pregnant woman who is addicted exists. Very much indeed may be at stake for her future child, and coercion of the pregnant woman, for the sake of her future child, is not paternalist. To this it could be added that, when, through a choice of lifestyle, she puts her future child at risk, she *actively* hurts her future child. And, in more ordinary circumstances, people are not allowed actively to hurt each other.

The woman who wants to carry on with her lifestyle might perhaps argue that, even if the harm she does her future child is something she docs actively, the harm is not intended. The harm is, at most, something merely foreseen.

This putative answer is not satisfactory, however. Those who believe that sometimes we may be permitted to cause harm, even if the harm is not intended but merely foreseen, hold that certain rules of proportionality must be met.

It might be morally permissible to alleviate pain in a manner that shortens the life of a terminally ill and suffering patient (the harm foreseen, i.e. the shortening of the patient's life, is a modest one). Moreover, the action causing the harm in question (the alleviation of pain) is a very good action indeed. However, the harm a pregnant woman may do to her future child by abusing drugs may be considerable. Moreover, the action producing the harm, the abuse of drugs, is hardly innocent as such, at least not in the sense that the alleviation of pain is.

Yet, for all that, it seems to me that no coercion should take place in this context. The reasons for this claim are a bit shaky, however. I rely here on the observation that, if harm is to be prevented, and the ideal of judicial security be honoured, the coercive measures must take place *ex post*.

First of all, the behaviour of women who put their children at risk must be made criminal, by an act of law.

Second, the women who put their children at risk must be punished afterwards, when they have been convicted for their crime. And the punishment must be consistent with the right to physical integrity on the part of the person who undergoes it. It is hard to believe that such a preventive (punitive) system would be very effective.

A reason to believe that it would be ineffective is that these women are, after all, addicted to the use of drugs. In most cases, they want to change their lifestyle. They care for their future child. Yet, for all that, they cannot change their way of living. Then it is hardly likely that the threat that they be punished unless they change their lifestyle will succeed.

The side-effects of a system that punishes women for not taking proper care of their foetuses during pregnancy are likely to be problematic. The following point made by the American bioethicist, Bonnie Steinbock, seems to me well taken:

> Making adversaries out of mother and fetus is likely to result in more harm than good. Many women will avoid physicians altogether during pregnancy if failure to follow medical advice can result in forced treatment or involuntary confinement. We need to find other options that will protect babies without turning women into (in George Annas's apt phrase) 'fetal containers'.
>
> (1989: 33)

Furthermore, a system that singles out these women, stigmatises them and makes criminals of them, is likely to reinforce a kind of prejudice against them, that is already widespread in society. And these kinds of prejudice, creating in these women a lack of confidence in society, are an obstacle, when it comes to providing these women with the kind of help they and their future children so desperately need.

Medication and surgery

Not only is it possible for pregnant women to put their future children at risk by choosing a lifestyle that is detrimental to the foetus. They may put their future child at risk by refusing certain investigations as well. They may also put their future child at risk by refusing to take certain drugs (intended to prevent or cure diseases affecting, not they themselves, but the foetus they carry). They may even put their future child at risk by refusing surgery on the foetus. Should society force investigations and treatment upon them?

This problem is less likely to occur than the aforementioned problem with pregnant women who refuse to give up a lifestyle that is dangerous to the health of the future child. Most pregnant women do care for their future children. And while some have difficulties in changing their lifestyle in the best interest of their future child (since they are addicted to some drug, say), no similar problem exists with respect to invasive procedures, directed ultimately at their foetuses. As a matter of fact, most women agree to suffer harm and hardship in the best interests of their future children. After all, in their decision to carry their pregnancy to term they have already accepted to undergo hard labour.

However, there may well be some rare cases where women, for some reason or other, refuse, say, to undergo surgery, even though it is of the utmost importance to their future child that they do. They may stubbornly refuse to accept the fact that surgery is needed. They may demand healing instead of surgery. Or they may claim that, as a life project, they have chosen not to become involved in new, spectacular and extraordinary medical methods. They may refuse to undergo a Caesarean section, arguing that they want to give birth to their child in a 'natural' way, even if it means that they knowingly jeopardise the life and health of their child.[3] How is society supposed to react to them?

It seems to be practice in many countries to force Caesareans on women in the best interest of the child. In many countries this kind of coercion is informal and never documented. However, in the US, where the cases sometimes go to court, we can see that this kind of coercion actually takes place. This is how Nancy K. Rhoden describes the situation:

> In the cases of which I am aware, every judge but one who has ruled on an application for nonconsensual Ceserean [sic] delivery has granted the request. Interestingly, *Roe* v. *Wade*, which has stood firmly for a woman's right to privacy and right to make her own decisions about pregnancy, is the case most commonly invoked by courts to justify these orders. Under *Roe*, women must be allowed to choose abortion prior to fetal viability. . . . But once a fetus is capable of independent life outside the womb, albeit with artificial aid, the state's interest in potential life becomes compelling. . . . Courts invoking *Roe* to support nonconsensual Cesarean delivery reason that since states can prohibit the intentional termination of fetal life after viability, they can likewise protect viable fetuses by preventing vaginal delivery when it will have the same effect as abortion.
>
> (1987: 33)

These women may well complain that, if they are coerced into accepting the measures they do not agree to, then they are treated unfairly. The harm they do, they do very indirectly and passively, they may point out. They may even falsely believe that they do no harm at all. And society does not require other persons, in other situations, to give up their life projects in order to help others. In particular, we are not required to give up our life projects in order to help strangers. But these women, if they agree that they allow harm to take place at all, may well argue that their future children are (just like) strangers to them.

---

3 A recent treatment, of this problem, from a legal point of view, can be found in Aurora Plomer, 'Judicially Enforced Caesareans and the Sanctity of Life' (1997).

Recall also that, if we want to coerce these women, and if we want to abide by the ideal of respect for judicial security, we must punish them for not helping their future children. It is out of the question, in a civilised society, to force the treatment upon them. These women, like all of us, have the right to physical integrity.

Could it not be argued, however, that these women have a special duty towards their future children? After all, if they have become pregnant, and if they have accepted their pregnancy and decided to carry it to term, then they have taken responsibility for the foetus/future child. They are not in the situation of an ordinary citizen in a rich country with respect to the poor in the Third World, but, rather, in the situation of the lifeguard, who passively observes when a person drowns.

This seems to be how US judges argue, when enforcing Caesareans with reference to *Roe* v. *Wade*. As a matter of fact, this argument has been a focus of the discussion about foetal/maternal conflicts and it has been discussed in, among other places, D. Mathieu's instructive monograph, *Preventing Prenatal Harm: Should the State Intervene?* (1991). In some ways, there is something in this simile, and in some ways not.

What bears out the simile is that, for *most* mothers-to-be, to decide not to have an abortion *is* to assume responsibility for the future child. This is how most mothers-to-be themselves conceive of the situation. So there is some sense in *holding* them responsible for the health of the future child too.

What runs against the simile, however, is that not *all* women conceive in this manner of the choice not to have an abortion. Some feel that, once they have become pregnant, they are trapped. This is because they do not believe in any right to abortion. They believe that abortion is wrong, period.

It would be very wrong for society to argue with respect to these latter kind of women that, since they have assumed responsibility for their future child, they must submit to such things as invasive investigations and even surgery. These women have simply not assumed any responsibility whatever with respect to the future child. The act of conception may have come close to rape. Once pregnant, there was nothing these women could do to get rid of the foetus. Their relation to it is not the same as the relation between the lifeguard and the drowning person. It is more like the relation between an ordinary person living in an industrially developed country and a starving person in a distant country.

Now, since it is not possible for a judge to distinguish these two cases, no coercion should take place at all. Pregnant women should be encouraged to undergo treatment, if the treatment is not too dangerous to them and is of importance to the health of their future child. However, no coercive measures should be taken in those very rare cases where a pregnant woman does not agree to be treated. Nor should she be punished for her refusal. Such coercion is not compatible with a respect for the ideal of judicial security.

If these women should be punished, then we should all be punished because of all sorts of omissions we commit, with very serious consequences for others. But we are not thus punished. So there is no reason to single out pregnant women exclusively, in an act of law. This would be to flout the ideal of judicial security (the requirement of consequentiality).

Moreover, this abstention from the use of coercion is so much more reasonable, since the cases where women refuse to undergo treatment that is indicated because of the medical needs of their foetus/future children, are so extremely rare.

Conclusion

Quite a few women put the health of their future child at risk by adopting a lifestyle that is dangerous for it. They use drugs and they smoke during pregnancy and they refuse to, or are simply not capable of, changing their habits.

Other women put the health of their future children at risk through inaction. They refuse to undergo invasive measures in the interests of their future child. They may refuse to believe that the measures are really in the best interests of their future child, or simply claim that, as a central life project, they have chosen not to be involved in extraordinary and spectacular methods of modern medicine, including Caesareans.

A strong presumption exists for coercing these women, in the interests of their future children, to change lifestyle or to undergo necessary medical measures. However, we ought to resist the temptation to do so, or so I have argued.

The main reason why we should resist the temptation to allow society (doctors, or social workers, or judges) to coerce these women is that, if such coercion is supposed to take place, it must take place in a manner compatible with a respect for the ideal of judicial security. But then it must take place *ex post*, in the form of punishment directed at women who break the law and do not change their lifestyle or do not accept necessary medical measures.

In the former case, i.e. in relation to women who abuse drugs, it is hard to see that the system would really have any preventive effect. After all, we are here dealing mainly with women who are addicted and who cannot change their lifestyle. If education and encouragement have failed, then there is little reason to believe that the threat of punishment would do the trick any better.

In the latter case, i.e. in relation to women who refuse surgery or medication, the requirement of consequentiality discussed in Chapter 1 forces us, if we want to punish women who do harm indirectly, through their inaction, to punish all people who, through inaction, do equal or worse harm. This means, probably, that every one in industrially advanced countries must be punished for not giving away (enough) money to famine relief. This is hardly feasible.

I do not want to say that people living in rich countries should not give away more of our wealth to famine relief. As a matter of fact, I think we ought to do so.[4] However, the method of achieving this kind of behaviour is not through punishment. This should be fairly obvious. But then, neither is the best way of achieving compliance by pregnant mothers in medical programmes designed to suit the interests of their future children to punish those who refuse to comply. Instead, these women should be *educated* and *encouraged* to comply.

In the rare cases when women do not yield to medical reason, we (and their future children) simply have to live with this failure.

---

4 An interesting argument to this effect can be found in Peter Unger's book, *Living High and Letting Die* (1996).

8

COERCION IN THE SOCIAL
SERVICES

Two kinds of coercion are common in the social services. On the one hand, people who misuse drugs are in some European countries compulsorily treated. The same is true in many US states. On the other hand, when children are either not taken care of properly by their parents, or themselves put their life and health in jeopardy through their selected lifestyle, society takes custody of them, from their parents.

The latter kind of compulsion has been touched upon in Chapter 2, in relation to somatic health care, where parents refuse life-saving treatment for their children; it will not be dealt with any further in the present book. In more ordinary circumstances it is an example of *coercion*, but not an example of coercive *care*. The former kind of coercion (against people for their drug abuse) will be discussed, however.

This former kind of coercive care against drug abuse takes different forms in the US and in different European countries. In the US, substance abuse was a crime until 1962 when the Supreme Court ruled that it was unconstitutional to prosecute a person for the status of being a drug-dependent person rather than for a criminal act (*Robinson* v. *California*, 370 USA 660 (1962)). The court said further, however, that the states could require addicts to undergo compulsory treatment. Around thirty states authorise civil commitment for substance abuse (Beck 1996: 15).

Some European countries are restrictive. For example, in England and Wales, the Netherlands and Spain, compulsory admission of abusers of alcohol or drugs will only take place in the case that the abuser has committed a crime. Let me refer to this as the Laissez-Faire Model.

In Sweden, on the other hand, a special Act on Compulsory Admission to Special Institutions for Abusers, allows coercive care as soon as (1) the abuser exposes his or her physical or mental health to a severe risk, (2) there is an obvious risk that he or she is ruining his or her life or (3) there is a danger that he or she will hurt him- or herself or some relative. Decision is taken by the administrative court. The abuser can be detained for up to six months. Let me refer to this as the Coercive Model.

Many countries occupy places in the middle of the continuum with the extreme points set by, on the one hand, countries like England and Wales, the Netherlands and Spain, coming close to the Laissez-Faire Model, and, on the other hand, many US states as well as Sweden, with their Coercive Model. In Finland and Denmark, for example, people may be subjected to a short period of coercive care, intended to make them sober up and decide whether to undergo further treatment on a voluntary basis.

The subject of coercive care in relation to drug abuse is not taken up explicitly in the Convention. The reason for this is obvious. The differences between European countries, the US, Canada, Japan and Australia are so great that it would be pointless to state a 'common denominator' in the field.

However, the question of what kind of practice is sound is real. It will be dealt with in the present chapter.

Should drug abusers be coercively treated against their abuse?

Would compulsory admission of drug abusers and coercive treatment of them against their abuse violate the principle of respect for the autonomy of the individual in decisions about medical care and social services?

I think it would, but this is debatable. Those who deny my claim might want to argue as follows.

A person who abuses drugs typically does so compulsively. He or she cannot avoid the drug. So when he or she is compulsorily admitted and coercively treated against his or her abuse, this does not flout the principle. The person in question cannot make an autonomous decision to give up the abuse. Society can act on the presumption that what it provides for this person is what he or she really wants.

We should resist this line of argument for two somewhat different reasons.

First of all, it is controversial whether drug abuse really needs to take a compulsive form. Is it true that a drug addict does not have it in his or her *power* to abstain from the drug? Or, is this rather something which is very *difficult* for the person to do? Or, is it *merely* a matter of motivation? Is the reason that the 'addict' goes on with his or her use that this is what he or she really wants to do?

According to some scientists, the use is often compulsive, according to others it rarely or never is.[1] Of course, this is not the place to try to settle this dispute. We should note, however that it does exist.

---

1 A review of experimental studies questioning the idea that drug addiction is strictly speaking 'compulsive' is given in M. Pattison *et al.*, *Emerging Concepts of Alcohol Dependence* (1977). I owe this reference to Anders Bergmark.

Second, and rather more important, even if it is true that a typical drug abuser cannot stop using the drug, i.e. even if it is true that a typical drug abuser cannot make an *effective* decision to give up the use of the drug (it is true, that is, that he or she cannot make an autonomous decision, as this notion was explained in Chapter 1, to give up the use of the drug), it may very well be true of him or her that he or she is capable of deciding whether to *join a certain programme* aimed at curing his or her addiction.

All this means that, if we want to hold on to the principle of respect for the autonomy of the individual in decisions about medical care and social services, we must avoid the Coercive Model.

As a matter of fact, the Coercive Model is unacceptable on two different counts.

First, the Coercive Model is unacceptable because it allows a person to be coercively treated against his or her drug addiction in the interest of *other* persons (close relatives). I have criticised this way of using treatment as a kind of punishment in the chapters about infectious disease and forensic psychiatry, and will say no more about it in the present context.

Second, the Coercive Model is not acceptable in that it merely assumes that drug-addicted persons cannot make autonomous decisions about whether to join a certain programme aimed at treating their addiction or not. If they do not suffer from delirium they are often perfectly capable of taking this kind of decision. In many cases they refuse to accept the suggested treatment, and their 'no' to the treatment should be taken for an answer.

However, does all this mean that we must accept the other extreme, and allow no compulsory treatment of drug addiction at all?

I think not. There is still room for some coercive treatment. In particular, there is room for the kind of coercion that takes place in countries like Finland and Denmark.

I think of coercion of a person who is suffering from delirium. This person is not, in the circumstances, capable of taking any autonomous decisions whatever. It is only fair to commit this person compulsorily for a short time, to help him or her to sober up, and to get rid of the delirium. A law making room for this kind of coercion could mean that people who are drug addicted are given a chance to get rid of their addiction. When they have sobered up they may be given the opportunity, voluntarily to join a programme against their abuse. Let me refer to this as the Emergency Model.

To the extent that this works out, and they agree to continue the treatment, everything is fine. And it is a good thing indeed that they have actively assented to the treatment. There is probably a therapeutic gain to be made from this.

However, is not this a bit naïve? Would not many just leave the programme, once they had sobered up and were given the opportunity to do so?

Well, probably many would. But then they were probably not motivated to end their abuse. So it is highly likely that all kinds of care, even coercive care, are ineffective in the situation.

However, even a person who sobers up, decides to join a certain programme to combat his or her abuse, is likely to give up the programme before it has succeeded. So should there be no room for any coercive measures against these people, as soon as they have agreed to participate in the programme? Should there be no way for those in charge of the programme to hold on to them, when they only too easily want to give up the cure?

I think there should be such possibilities. To this effect I need to introduce a final kind of permissible coercion: Ulyssian coercion.

Ulyssian coercion

As we remember, Ulysses had his sailors tie him to the mast of his ship, in order to render it impossible for him to yield to the sirens' song. It should be possible to do something similar for people who want to give up their addiction, and who believe that a certain programme against it will be effective, but foresee that they will not be capable of carrying through the entire programme voluntarily. They should be offered the possibility of making a contract. The terms of the contract would be as follows. For a certain limited time a certain institution should be permitted (indeed, obliged) to keep them, if necessary against their will, and submit them to the desired treatment. If they protested and claimed that they had changed their mind, this would not affect the policy of the institution. The institution would refer to the contract and continue to treat them for their abuse, in the manner described in the contract.

The reason for allowing for this possibility should be obvious. We all suffer from weakness of will (*akrasia*) to some extent. And in many situations we take precautions to ascertain that we will not yield to future temptations. We use our friends to this effect, urging them to take us home from the party before it degenerates and we make a fool of ourselves; we even vote for laws making the use of such things as safety belts compulsory, because we know that, otherwise, in many situations, we will not use them. So why should not dug addicts be allowed to take precautions against their weakness of will which, in relation to the drug, may come close to compulsiveness?

Yet, for all that, this exception from the rule that coercive care should not be given is problematic. There is no denying that it flouts the principle of respect for the autonomy of the individual in decisions about medical care and social services, as it was stated in Chapter 1. After all, I have been stressing that it is the *actual* wish of a person, when such a wish can be ascertained, that should be honoured. I have stressed that a person should be allowed to change his or her mind about a certain treatment, once it has been consented to.

This is also stressed in the Convention. In Article 5, stating that an intervention in the health field may only be carried out after the person concerned has given free and informed consent to it, it is stressed that: 'The person concerned may freely withdraw consent at any time.' So if the person concerned is capable of making an autonomous decision, decides to leave the programme, but is not allowed to do so, then this is problematic indeed.

It might be argued that accepting Ulyssian coercion is no more problematic than accepting legally binding living wills, as I did in Chapter 3. However, there is an important difference between these two cases. When the time comes to execute a living will, the person who wrote the will is no longer capable of exercising any will or, at least, he or she is not capable of communicating their wishes. To be sure, this person may have changed his or her mind. However, we cannot know this for sure. And the person knew, when he or she wrote the will, that it would be respected. Then it is acceptable to respect it, in spite of the *possibility* that in so doing one may come to act against the present will of the patient.

The situation is very different when Ulyssian coercion is practised. We then *know* that we act against the present will of the addicted client/patient.

However, it might be argued, there are other situations in life where people, because of contracts, are forced to do things against their present will. Even if health care is special, these situations may be of the utmost importance to these persons. What they have to do may seem to them, now that they have to do it, abhorrent, and yet, for all that, they have to go through with it. So perhaps it is not too serious if people are also allowed to contract away some of their future autonomy in relation to health care.

This argument is not convincing. If I contract to be at a certain place at a certain time in the future and then change my mind and never show up, then the person with whom I have the contract may *sue* me for not showing up; he or she may not, however, have the police fetch me. Nor is he or she allowed to make me come to the place. However, this is exactly what is done to a person who is submitted to Ulyssian coercion.

For these reasons I am reluctant to make an exception from the principle of respect for the autonomy of the individual in decisions about medical care and social services and allow that Ulyssian coercion take place. However, I realise that this kind of coercion may be what some people desperately need. And it does not seem right to deny them the possibility of making these kinds of contracts. So in the final analysis I feel that I must conclude that such coercion may be warranted.

I make this concession only in relation to the treatment of drug abuse, however. And, once again, I make it reluctantly.

There is a risk that such an exception, if it took the form of law, would be just the first step towards a situation where more systematic violations of the principle would be tolerated. And yet, for all that, I think we should try out the possibility, being prepared to give it up, if it turns out to work rather in the manner we feared than in the manner we had hoped for.

Should criminals be forced to give up their drug abuse?

In some countries, such as England and Wales, the Netherlands and Spain, people who have been convicted for crimes related to drug abuse are being coercively treated for their abuse. Is *this* practice acceptable?

It is not. A person who has been convicted, say, of drunken driving may be informed that, if he or she joins a certain programme against his or her abuse, and concludes it successfully, this may affect the assessment of their dangerousness. If the person can prove him- or herself less dangerous, through successes in the programme, then this may lead to release from prison. If this is merely a true piece of information, then it is not objectionable to provide it. And I have already argued, in Chapter 6 about forensic psychiatric care, that a legitimate ground for releasing people from prison may be that we assess them as less dangerous than we did when we put them there.

However, when a person is *forced* to join a programme against his or her drug abuse, then this is objectionable. Neither should he or she be *punished* for refusing to join the programme (as is being done when something extra is added to the punishment if the person does not comply with the programme). Not even positive rewards should be allowed. Such measures mean that the treatment against the addiction will be seriously compromised. In this, treatment of drug addiction is no different from treatment of mental illness, psychopathology, sexual abnormality and so forth.

But *is* it coercion to offer a person release from prison, if he or she successfully concludes a programme aimed at curing his or her addiction?

It is not, it seems to me, if the crucial thing is whether the person does prove less dangerous, after having concluded the treatment. Compliance with the programme *as such* should not lead to a shorter punishment. This would be objectionable. But the success of the programme, documented somehow, could legitimately result in a shortened punishment.

If some treatment exists then, it should be offered to the criminal, but only on a voluntary basis. If the criminal complies with the treatment, then this should not mean automatically that he or she will be released (any earlier). However, if he or she does comply with the programme, and, after having done so, turns out to be less dangerous, then *this* may be a

134

legitimate (and perfectly reasonable) ground for setting him or her free earlier, on parole, say.

Does it matter whether coercive care is effective?

I have argued for a restrictive use of coercive care in relation to drug abuse and for a restrictive use only. The only use of coercion I accept is coercion of people who, because they hallucinate or suffer from delirium, are not capable of reaching any autonomous decisions whatever, and what I have called Ulyssian coercion, exercised because it has been licensed by the client through a contract. This restrictive view is mainly to do with the fact that a more inclusive view must come to flout the principle of respect for the autonomy of the individual in decisions about medical care and social services in a serious manner.

Something that may seem to make my position even more plausible is perhaps the fact that it is doubtful whether coercive care against drug abuse is really effective. There are even those who question whether any kind of therapy for drug abuse is effective. When people give up their addiction – and many do – this is not because of therapy of any kind, but because of changed motivation, or simply because the disease (if the drug abuse is a disease) has healed and disappeared. And there are even some results indicating that coercive care may sometimes increase, rather than decrease, mortality among drug addicts. Now, even setting these rather extreme results to one side, it may seem very problematic indeed to coerce people into accepting a care of doubtful effect.[2]

How can society accept people being coerced when it is doubtful whether there is any positive effect at all associated with the coercion? How can society accept people being coerced when it is hard even to exclude the possibility that the care coercively given to these people is positively detrimental to them?

There may be something to this argument, but I do not want to rely on it in my rejection of coercive care. For suppose that it emerged that, contrary to what seems now to be part of the received opinion, a (new) kind of therapy proved *extremely* effective. Would this provide us with a reason to permit this therapy to be given coercively? I think not.

---

2 A standard review of studies of the effectiveness of treatment against drug addiction is W.R. Miller, 'The Effectiveness of Treatment for Substance Abuse' (1992). Now, Miller has some hopes for the future. In particular, he believes that, when kind of treatment and kind of person treated are better matched, good results will be forthcoming. This conjecture seems not to have been born out by realities. At least this is what is claimed by Anders Bergmark, who informed me of Miller's study. Bergmark points out that Miller's optimism about the future was based on a conjecture that has, as yet, not been confirmed. Bergmark's discussion is found (in Swedish) in, 'Ett lik i lasten?' (1994).

First, we must investigate how this therapy works. If it drastically changes the personality of the drug addicted clients/patients, this may be problematic in itself. It may be even more problematic when coercion is added to the cure. This would come close to the coercive exchange of certain people for other people. Such therapy might be considered a threat to the very (personal) existence of the clients/patients. It would definitely flout Article 1 of the Convention, where it is stated:

> Parties to this Convention shall protect the dignity and identity of all human beings and guarantee everyone, without discrimination, respect for their integrity and other rights and fundamental freedoms with regard to the application of biology and medicine.

Even if this may sound eccentric, I do not want to say that it might not be a good thing to be exchanged for some other creature, better suited to live a good life than I am.[3] However, such an exchange is, as a matter of fact, feared by most people. And there are even some philosophers arguing that it would be an evil. So if society allows it to take place, the popular trust in relation to health care and social authorities will be ruined. And *this* would mean a definite loss to society as such.

Second, even if the therapy did not change the personality of the drug-addicted client/patient, but just stopped the abuse, perhaps because of a chemical reaction of some kind, I would still be sceptical of allowing coercion to take place. Suppose the drug, when combined with a certain medicine, was no longer experienced as pleasant by the former abuser. Would it now be acceptable coercively to give the client/patient the medicine, in order to stop the abuse? I think not.

If such a medicine existed, it would provide a very good means for those who wanted to give up their abuse to do so. Most abusers would perhaps choose to take the medicine in question. However, if there were some residual ones, who did not want to take the medicine, in spite of the fact that they knew that it would work, and that it would work without any bad side-effects, then we must come to suspect that these people, contrary to what we at first believed, may have some good reasons to go on with their abuse.

As a matter of fact, the word 'abuse' may now turn out to be a misnomer. For even if the use of drugs is detrimental to their health, the possibility exists that, on the whole, it adds to the quality of their lives.

Who are we to judge? After all, it is not us but these persons themselves who have a privileged position, and a special interest, with respect to the lives they live.

---

3 I discuss this possibility in Chapter 7 of my *Hedonistic Utilitarianism* (1998).

Conclusion

People who become addicted to some drug may become, through misuse of the drug, temporarily incapable of reaching any decision about their own medical needs. If they are not capable of reaching an autonomous decision, but need care desperately (for their own sake), they should be compulsorily admitted to an institution capable of taking care of them.

However, no one should be compulsorily admitted because this is what any one *else* needs (their close relatives, or society at large).

Moreover, once the delirium has gone away, once these people are capable of reaching an autonomous decision, their right to a veto against treatment should be respected. Coercive care given in this way is what is demanded by what I have called the Emergency Model.

It is a moot question, we have seen, whether there exists such a thing as a truly compulsive use of drugs. However, it is obviously very *difficult* for some people, who have become addicted to a drug, to give up their use of the drug. These people may know that, even if they voluntarily join a pro-gramme aimed at treating them, they will give it up before they are cured. These people should be allowed voluntarily to *contract* into (future) coercive care, on a temporary basis. For obvious reasons, I have called this Ulyssian coercion. And I take the Emergency Model to allow also for Ulyssian coercion.

It seems to me that, for humanitarian reasons, Ulyssian coercion is inescapable. Yet, for all that, it is at variance with the principle of respect for the autonomy of the individual in decisions about medical care and social services, so I have only hesitantly accepted it. If too generously used, I feel that it might put us on a slippery slope, where the most basic values defended in this book are put in jeopardy.

9

CONCLUSION

In this book I have stated a principle of respect for the autonomy of the individual in decisions about medical care and social services, based on two ideals, one anti-paternalist and one concerning judicial security. I have conjectured that, if we had laws regulating coercive care that respect this principle, then we would have good laws. On the whole, these laws would mean that as few lives as possible were lost in health care and social services and, furthermore, that a widespread trust in the health care and social system could evolve.

Has my conjecture been born out by realities? To the extent that my argument is correct, and with three caveats, it has.

I have confronted existing Western laws of a wide variety, covering the entire health care field as well as the social services with my principle, and I have found that, when, as often, there has been a conflict between existing laws and my principle, the law at variance with the principle should yield.

I have argued that if laws regulating coercion in somatic health care, preventive health care, the defence against infectious disease, mental illness, forensic psychiatry, foetal/maternal conflicts, and the social services, were to live up to the demands of the principle, they would be acceptable. However, there are three caveats.

First, I have noted that existing laws and practices concerning the prevention of suicide in all European countries, in the US, Canada and Australia, flout the ideal of anti-paternalism. I have adumbrated a system that would eliminate this problem, if it could be adopted. This is the system of suicide clinics, discussed in Chapter 2. However, I am reluctant to advocate that suicide clinics be introduced.

I have no definite stand on this issue. I have found no way of ascertaining whether some conditions highly relevant in this context could be fulfilled. In particular, I have not been able to tell whether such clinics would strengthen, or rather counteract, the systematic attempts at suicide prevention which are of central importance to the entire health care system. So I have to leave it as unfinished business whether the principle of respect for the autonomy of the individual in decisions about medical care and social services can be fully applied to the problem of suicide prevention.

Second, I have noted that in the treatment of people who suffer from mental impairment or senile dementia, there is no principled stance that society can take up, that fully satisfies both the ideal of anti-paternalism and the ideal of judicial security. For want of anything better I have here come to advocate a systematic hypocrisy, where the laws forbid all kinds of coercion with respect to these patients, while some coercion (I have called it 'modest coercion') is still expected to be forthcoming, while another kind of coercion (I have called it 'meddlesome coercion') is supposed not to take place. I am not at all happy with this proposal, but I have simply not been able to think of anything better.

Finally, in my treatment of coercion in the social services I have noted that there seems to exist an urgent need for a certain kind of coercion where a person suffering from drug abuse contracts, at one time, not to be allowed, later on, to leave a certain programme, aimed at curing his or her drug addiction. I have called this kind of coercion 'Ulyssian coercion'. There is no doubt that this kind of coercion, if it were allowed to take place, would flout the principle of respect for the autonomy of the individual in decisions about medical care and social services. Yet, for all that, I have come to defend the position that, for humanitarian reasons, it takes place.

I suppose this final 'defeat' of my argument is only what should have been expected. No matter how hard you try to get things straight, if you are sensitive to the demands of reality, you will always be forced into *some* kind of (intellectual) compromise. I console myself with the reflection that this compromise is only a small and isolated one. The *main* thrust of my argument in this book, it seems to me, has proved sound.

In many cases discussed in this book I have taken sides. Here are some examples.

I have defended the liberal procreation laws in countries like the US, the UK, France and Italy, denouncing the restrictive laws of the Nordic countries, especially the laws of Norway and Sweden.

I have defended the kind of stance taken towards infectious disease by countries like the Netherlands and France, denouncing the kind of stance taken by several North American states as well as Sweden.

And I have defended the kind of stance taken towards drug-addicted people adopted by countries like Denmark and Finland – the Emergency Model – denouncing a much too restrictive use of coercion in countries like the Netherlands and Spain, as well as a much too inclusive use of coercion in a country like Sweden and in many US states.

I have defended the right to physical integrity of pregnant women, even if this means that, in some cases, some women will actively hurt their future children by adopting a certain lifestyle, or that, in other circumstances, some women will allow that the life and health of their future children be put at risk by their refusal to undergo treatment in the interest of their future children, denouncing the legal systems to the opposite effect that seem presently to be forthcoming especially in North America, but not practised in Western Europe.

Being an independent thinker, with no loyalties to anything but my own criteria of scientific rigour and moral sense, this partisan stance has not proved difficult. However, there are two important cases where I have not been able to take sides. In these cases I have advocated stances adopted by *no* countries whatever. I think of my treatment of coercive psychiatric care.

I realise that my proposal that the sole legitimate ground for compulsorily committing people to psychiatric treatment be their need for the treatment in combination with their incapability of deciding for themselves – the Incompetency Model – leaving the decision about detaining them to the court, is *somewhat* controversial. And I realise that my proposal that people who have committed crimes under the influence of mental illness be put into prison – the Full Responsibility Model – is *very* controversial indeed. It is not likely that these proposals will become actual law in the near future, I must concede. However, there are extremely good reasons for each of them, and, in particular, for the two of them in combination, or so I have argued.

There seems to be no other way for the industrially developed societies in the Western world to live up to both the principle of respect for the autonomy of the individual in decisions about medical care and social services, and for the psychiatrists in these societies to satisfy the requirements of the Declaration of Hawaii, than by these societies adopting my proposals about coercive psychiatric treatment and forensic psychiatry. Unless they do so, these states will also have problems ratifying the Convention (stating that people may only be committed to psychiatric treatment if this is what they *themselves* need).

So I conclude this book in the hope that my proposals of the Incompetency Model (for civil commitment) and the Full Responsibility Model (for forensic psychiatric care) will provoke some discussion and, eventually, in due time, contribute to a general change of view. A sharp demarcation line *should* be drawn between, on the one hand, punishment and, on the other hand, care.

Appendix

CONVENTION ON HUMAN RIGHTS AND BIOMEDICINE

Here follows the Convention on Human Rights and Biomedicine, many times referred to in this book, adopted by the Committee of Ministers in the Council of Europe on 19 November 1996,[1] open to signature by the Member States of the Council of Europe, the Non-Member States which have participated in its elaboration (Australia, Canada, the Holy See, Japan and the United States of America), and by the European Community.

Preamble

The Member States of the Council of Europe, the other States and the European Community signatories hereto,

Bearing in mind the Universal Declaration of Human Rights proclaimed by the General Assembly of the United Nations on 10 December 1948;

Bearing in mind the Convention for the Protection of Human Rights and Fundamental Freedoms of 4 November 1950;

Bearing in mind the European Social Charter of 18 October 1961;

Bearing in mind the International Convenant on Civil and Political Rights and the International Convenant on Economic, Social and Cultural Rights of 16 December 1966;

Bearing in mind the Convention for the Protection of Individuals with regard to Automatic Processing of Personal Data of 28 January 1981;

Bearing also in mind the Convention on the Rights of the Child of 20 November 1989;

---

1 Germany, Belgium and Poland abstained when the Committee of Ministers took the vote on the adoption of the Convention.

Considering that the aim of the Council of Europe is the achievement of a greater unity between its members and that one of the methods by which that aim is to be pursued is the maintenance and further realisation of human rights and fundamental freedoms;

Conscious of the accelerating developments in biology and medicine;

Convinced of the need to respect the human being both as an individual and as a member of the human species and recognising the importance of ensuring the dignity of the human being;

Conscious that the misuse of biology and medicine may lead to acts endangering human dignity;

Affirming that progress in biology and medicine should be used for the benefit of present and future generations;

Stressing the need for international co-operation so that all humanity may enjoy the benefits of biology and medicine;

Recognising the importance of promoting a public debate on the questions posed by the application of biology and medicine and the responses to be given thereto;

Wishing to remind all members of society of their rights and responsibilities;

Taking account of the work of the Parliamentary Assembly in this field, including Recommendation 1160 (1991) on the preparation of a Convention on bioethics;

Resolving to take such measures as are necessary to safeguard human dignity and the fundamental rights and freedoms of the individual with regard to the application of biology and medicine;

Have agreed as follows:

Chapter I – general provisions

Article 1 – purpose and object

Parties to this Convention shall protect the dignity and identity of all human beings and guarantee everyone, without discrimination, respect for their integrity and other rights and fundamental freedoms with regard to the application of biology and medicine.

Each Party shall take in its internal law the necessary measures to give effect to the provisions of this Convention.

Article 2 – primacy of the human being

The interests and welfare of the human being shall prevail over the sole interest of society or science.

Article 3 – equitable access to health care

Parties, taking into account health needs and available resources, shall take appropriate measures with a view to providing, within their jurisdiction, equitable access to health care of appropriate quality.

Article 4 – professional standards

Any intervention in the health field, including research, must be carried out in accordance with relevant professional obligations and standards.

Chapter II – consent

Article 5 – general rule

An intervention in the health field may only be carried out after the person concerned has given free and informed consent to it.

This person shall beforehand be given appropriate information as to the purpose and nature of the intervention as well as on its consequences and risks.

The person concerned may freely withdraw consent at any time.

Article 6 – protection of persons not able to consent

(1) Subject to Articles 17 and 20 below, an intervention may only be carried out on a person who does not have the capacity to consent, for his or her direct benefit.

(2) Where, according to law, a minor does not have the capacity to consent to an intervention, the intervention may only be carried out with the

authorisation of his or her representative or an authority or a person or body provided for by law.

The opinion of the minor shall be taken into consideration as an increasingly determining factor in proportion to his or her age and degree of maturity.

(3) Where, according to law, an adult does not have the capacity to consent to an intervention because of a mental disability, a disease or for similar reasons, the intervention may only be carried out with the authorisation of his or her representative or an authority or a person or body provided for by law.

The individual concerned shall as far as possible take part in the authorisation procedure.

(4) The representative, the authority, the person or the body mentioned in paragraphs 2 and 3 above shall be given, under the same conditions, the information referred to in Article 5.

(5) The authorisation referred to in paragraphs 2 and 3 above may be withdrawn at any time in the best interests of the person concerned.

Article 7 – protection of persons who have mental disorder

Subject to protective conditions prescribed by law, including supervisory, control and appeal procedures, a person who has a mental disorder of a serious nature may be subjected, without his or her consent, to an intervention aimed at treating his or her mental disorder only where, without such treatment, serious harm is likely to result to his or her health.

Article 8 – emergency situation

When because of an emergency situation the appropriate consent cannot be obtained, any medically necessary intervention may be carried out immediately for the benefit of the health of the individual concerned.

Article 9 – previously expressed wishes

The previously expressed wishes relating to a medical intervention by a patient who is not, at the time of the intervention, in a state to express his or her wishes shall be taken into account.

Chapter III – private life and right to information

Article 10 – private life and right to information

(1) Everyone has the right to respect for private life in relation to information about his or her health.

(2) Everyone is entitled to know any information collected about his or her health. However, the wishes of individuals not to be so informed shall be observed.

(3) In exceptional cases, restrictions may be placed by law on the exercise of the rights contained in paragraph 2 in the interests of the patient.

Chapter IV – human genome

Article 11 – non-discrimination

Any form of discrimination against a person on grounds of his or her genetic heritage is prohibited.

Article 12 – predictive tests

Tests which are predictive of genetic diseases or which serve either to identify the subject as a carrier of a gene responsible for a disease or to detect a genetic predisposition or susceptibility to a disease may be performed only for health purposes or for scientific research linked to health purposes, and subject to appropriate genetic counselling.

Article 13 – interventions on the human genome

An intervention seeking to modify the human genome may only be undertaken for preventive, diagnostic or therapeutic purposes and only if its aim is not to introduce any modification on the genome of any descendants.

Article 14 – non-selection of sex

The use of techniques of medically assisted procreation shall not be allowed for the purpose of choosing a future child's sex, except where serious hereditary sex-related disease is to be avoided.

Chapter V – scientific research

Article 15 – general rule

Scientific research in the field of biology and medicine shall be carried out freely, subject to the provisions of this Convention and the other legal provisions ensuring the protection of the human being.

Article 16 – protection of persons undergoing research

Research on a person may only be undertaken if all the following conditions are met:

(i)   there is no alternative of comparable effectiveness to research on humans,

(ii) the risks which may be incurred by that person are not disproportionate to the potential benefits of the research,

(iii) the research project has been approved by the competent body after independent examination of its scientific merit, including assessment of the importance of the aim of the research, and multidisciplinary review of its ethical acceptability,

(iv) the persons undergoing research have been informed of their rights and the safeguards prescribed by law for their protection,

(v)   the necessary consent as provided for under Article 5 has been given expressly, specifically and is documented. Such consent may be freely withdrawn at any time.

Article 17 – protection of persons not able to consent to research

(1) Research on a person without the capacity to consent as stipulated in Article 5 may be undertaken only if all the following conditions are met:

(i)   the conditions laid down in Article 16, sub-paragraphs i to iv, are fulfilled;

(ii) the results of the research have the potential to produce real and direct benefit to his or her health;

(iii) research of comparable effectiveness cannot be carried out on individuals capable of giving consent;

(iv) the necessary authorisation provided for under Article 6 has been given specifically and in writing, and

(v)   the person concerned does not object.

(2) Exceptionally and under the protective conditions prescribed by law, where the research has not the potential to produce results of direct benefit to the health of the person concerned, such research may be authorised subject to the conditions laid down in paragraph 1, sub-paragraphs i, iii, iv and v above, and to the following additional conditions:

(i)   the research has the aim of contributing, through significant improvement in the scientific understanding of the individual's condition, disease or disorder, to the ultimate attainment of results capable of conferring benefit to the person concerned or to other persons in the same age category or afflicted with the same disease or disorder or having the same condition;

(ii) the research entails only minimal risk and minimal burden for the individual concerned.

Article 18 – research on embryos in vitro

(1) Where the law allows research on embryos in vitro, it shall ensure adequate protection of the embryo.

(2) The creating of human embryos for research purposes is prohibited.

Chapter VI – organ and tissue removal from living donors for transplantation purposes

Article 19 – general rule

(1) Removal of organs or tissue from a living person for transplantation purposes may be carried out solely for the therapeutic benefit of the recipient and where there is no suitable organ or tissue available from a deceased person and no other alternative therapeutic method of comparable effectiveness.

(2) The necessary consent as provided for under Article 5 must have been given expressly and specifically either in written form or before an official body.

Article 20 – protection of persons not able to consent to organ removal

(1) No organ or tissue removal may be carried out on a person who does not have the capacity to consent under Article 5.

(2) Exceptionally and under the protective conditions prescribed by law, the removal of regenerative tissue from a person who does not have the capacity to consent may be authorised provided the following conditions are met:

(i)   there is no compatible donor available who has the capacity to consent,
(ii) the recipient is a brother or sister of the donor,
(iii) the donation must have the potential to be life-saving for the recipient,
(iv) the authorisation provided for under paragraphs 2 and 3 of Article 6 has been given specifically and in writing, in accordance with the law and with the approval of the competent body,
(v)   the potential donor concerned does not object.

Chapter VII – prohibition of financial gain and disposal of a part of the human body

Article 21 – prohibition of financial gain

The human body and its parts shall not, as such, give rise to financial gain.

Article 22 – disposal of a removed part of the human body

When in the course of an intervention any part of a human body is removed, it may be stored and used for a purpose other than that for which it was removed, only if this is done in conformity with appropriate information and consent procedures.

Chapter VIII – infringements of the provisions of the Convention

Article 23 – infringement of the rights or principles

The Parties shall provide appropriate judicial protection to prevent or put a stop to an unlawful infringement of the rights and principles set forth in this Convention at short notice.

Article 24 – compensation for undue damage

The person who has suffered undue damage resulting from an intervention is entitled to fair compensation according to the conditions and procedures prescribed by law.

Article 25 – sanctions

Parties shall provide for appropriate sanctions to be applied in the event of infringement of the provisions contained in this Convention.

Chapter IX – relations between this Convention and other provisions

Article 26 – restrictions on the exercise of the rights

(1) No restrictions shall be placed on the exercise of the rights and protective provisions contained in this Convention other than such as are prescribed by law and are necessary in a democratic society in the interest of public safety, for the prevention of crime, for the protection of public health or for the protection of the rights and freedoms of others.

(2) The restrictions contemplated in the preceding paragraph may not be placed on Articles 11, 13, 14, 16, 17, 19, 20 and 21.

Article 27 – wider protections

None of the provisions of this Convention shall be interpreted as limiting or otherwise affecting the possibility for a Party to grant a wider measure of protection with regard to the application of biology and medicine than is stipulated in this Convention.

Chapter X – public debate

Article 28 – public debate

Parties to this Convention shall see to it that the fundamental questions raised by the developments of biology and medicine are the subject of appropriate public discussion in the light, in particular, of relevant medical, social, economic, ethical and legal implications, and that their possible application is made the subject of appropriate consultation.

Chapter XI – interpreting the Convention

Article 29 – interpretation of the Convention

The European Court of Human Rights may give, without direct reference to any specific proceedings pending in a court, advisory opinions on legal questions concerning the interpretation of the present Convention at the request of:

– the Government of a Party, after having informed the other Parties
– the Committee set up by Article 32, with membership restricted to the Representatives of the Parties to this Convention, by a decision adopted by a two-third majority of votes cast.

Article 30 – reports on the application of the Convention

On receipt of a request from the Secretary General of the Council of Europe any Party shall furnish an explanation of the manner in which its internal law ensures the effective implementation of any of the provisions of the Convention.

Chapter XII – protocols

Protocols may be concluded in pursuance of Article 32, with a view to developing, in specific fields, the principles contained in this Convention.

The Protocols shall be open for signature by Signatories of the Convention. They shall be subject to ratification, acceptance or approval. A signatory may not ratify, accept or approve Protocols without previously or simultaneously ratifying, accepting or approving the Convention.

Chapter XIII – amendments to the Convention

Article 32 – amendments to the Convention

(1) The tasks assigned to 'the Committee' in the present article and in Article 29 shall be carried out by the Steering Committee on Bioethics (CDBI), or by any other committee designated to do so by the Committee of Ministers.

(2) Without prejudice to the specific provisions of Article 29, each member State of the Council of Europe, as well as each Party to the present Convention which is not a member of the Council of Europe, may be represented and have one vote in the Committee when the Committee carries out the tasks assigned to it by the present Convention.

(3) Any State referred to in Article 33 or invited to accede to the Convention in accordance with the provisions of Article 34 which is not Party to this

Convention may be represented on the Committee by an observer. If the European Community is not a Party it may be represented on the Committee by an observer.

(4) In order to monitor scientific developments, the present Convention shall be examined within the Committee no later than five years from its entry into force and thereafter at such intervals as the Committee may determine.

(5) Any proposal for an amendment to this Convention, and any proposal for a Protocol or for an amendment to a Protocol, presented by a Party, the Committee or the Committee of Ministers shall be communicated to the Secretary General of the Council of Europe and forwarded by him to the member States of the Council of Europe, to the European Community, to any Signatory, to any Party, to any State invited to sign this Convention in accordance with the provisions of Article 33 and to any State invited to accede to it in accordance with the provisions of Article 34.

(6) The Committee shall examine the proposal not earlier than two months after it has been forwarded by the Secretary General in accordance with paragraph 5. The Committee shall submit the text adopted by a two thirds majority of the votes cast to the Committee of Ministers for approval. After its approval, this text shall be forwarded to the Parties for ratification, acceptance or approval.

(7) Any amendments shall enter into force, in respect of those Parties which have accepted it, on the first day of the month following the expiration of a period of one month after the date on which five Parties, including at least four member States of the Council of Europe, have informed the Secretary General that they have accepted it.

In respect of any Party which subsequently accepts it, the amendment shall enter into force on the first day of the month following the expiration of a period of one month after the date on which that Party has informed the Secretary General of its acceptance.

Chapter XIV – final clauses

Article 33 – signature, ratification and entry into force

(1) This Convention shall be open for signature by the member States of the Council of Europe, the non-member States which have participated in its elaboration and by the European Community.

(2) This Convention is subject to ratification, acceptance or approval. Instruments of ratification, acceptance or approval shall be deposited with the Secretary General of the Council of Europe.

(3) This Convention shall enter into force on the first day of the month following the expiration of a period of three months after the date on which five States, including at least four member States of the Council of Europe, have expressed their consent to be bound by the Convention in accordance with the previous of paragraph 2 of the present article.

(4) In respect of any Signatory which subsequently expresses its consent to be bound by it, the Convention shall enter into force on the first day of the month following the expiration of a period of three months after the date of the deposit of its instrument of ratification, acceptance or approval.

Article 34 – non-member States

(1) After the entry into force of this Convention, the Committee of Ministers of the Council of Europe may, after consultation of the Parties, invite any non-member State of the Council of Europe to accede to this Convention by a decision taken by the majority provided for in Article 20, sub-paragraph d, of the Statue of the Council of Europe, and by the unanimous vote of the representatives of the Contracting States entitled to sit on the Committee of Ministers.

(2) In respect of any acceding State, the Convention shall enter into force on the first day of the month following the expiration of a period of three months after the date of deposit of the instrument of accession with the Secretary General of the Council of Europe.

Article 35 – territories

(1) Any Signatory may, at the time of signature or when depositing its instrument of ratification, acceptance or approval, specify the territory or territories to which this Convention shall apply. Any other State may formu-late the same declaration when depositing its instrument of accession.

(2) Any Party may, at any later date, by a declaration addressed to the Secretary General of the Council of Europe, extend the application of this Convention to any other territory specified in the declaration and for whose international relations it is responsible or on whose behalf it is authorised to give undertakings. In respect of such territory the Convention shall enter

into force on the first day of the month following the expiration of a period of three months after the date of receipt of such declaration by the Secretary General.

(3) Any declaration made under the two preceding paragraphs may, in respect of any territory specified in such declaration, be withdrawn by a notification addressed to the Secretary General. The withdrawal shall become effective on the first day of the month following the expiration of a period of three months after the date of receipt of such modification by the Secretary General.

Article 36 – reservations

(1) Any State and the European Community may, when signing this Convention or when depositing the instrument of ratification, make a reservation in respect of any particular provision of the Convention to the extent that any law then in force in its territory is not in conformity with the provision. Reservations of a general character shall not be permitted under this article.

(2) Any reservation made under this article shall contain a brief statement of the relevant law.

(3) Any Party which extends the application of this Convention to a territory mentioned in the declaration referred to in Article 35, paragraph 2, may, in respect of the territory concerned, make a reservation in accordance with the provisions of the preceding paragraphs.

(4) Any Party which has made the reservation mentioned in this Article may withdraw it by means of a declaration addressed to the Secretary General of the Council of Europe. The withdrawal shall become effective on the first day of the month following the expiration of a period of one month after the date of its receipt by the Secretary General.

Article 37 – denunciation

(1) Any Party may at any time denounce this Convention by means of a notification addressed to the Secretary General of the Council of Europe.

(2) Such denunciation shall become effective on the first day of the month following the expiration of a period of three months after the date of receipt of the notification by the Secretary General.

Article 38 – notifications

The Secretary General of the Council of Europe shall notify the member States of the Council, the European Community, and Signatory, any Party and any other State which has been invited to accede to this Convention of:

(a) any signature;
(b) the deposit of any instrument of ratification, acceptance, approval or accession;
(c) any date of entry into force of this Convention in accordance with Articles 33 or 34;
(d) any amendment or Protocol adopted in accordance with Article 32, and the date on which such an amendment or Protocol enters into force;
(e) any declaration made under the provisions of Article 35;
(f) any reservation and withdrawal of reservation made in pursuance of the provisions of Article 36;
(g) any other act, notification or communication relating to this Convention.

In witness whereof the undersigned, being duly authorised thereto, have signed this Convention.

GLOSSARY

In this glossary some of the technical terms in this book are listed and explained.

Coercive Model (of treatment of drug abuse)   According to this model, people who through drug abuse put their own life and health in jeopardy (or the life and health of others, such as close relatives), should be coercively treated for their abuse.

Emergency Model (for treatment of drug abuse)   According to this model, people who through drug abuse put their own life and health in jeopardy and who are not capable of reaching an autonomous decision about their own need of treatment (because they suffer from delirium, say), ought to be coercively treated to a point where they can exercise an autonomous will. From then on they should not be submitted to coercive care, unless they opt for Ulyssian coercion.

Excuse Model (of forensic psychiatric care)   According to this model, people who commit crimes under the influence of mental illness are excused and considered unfit for trial. If they are dangerous, they are detained in the interest of the safety of the rest of the citizens. But this decision to detain them is taken independently of any judicial assessment of the crime they have committed and it is not founded upon any statute of criminal law. This model is rejected in the present book.

Full Responsibility Model (of forensic psychiatric care)   According to this model, people who commit crimes under the influence of mental illness are convicted in accordance with criminal law and sentenced to gaol (or whatever kind of punishment may be in order for the crime in question); however, if this is what they need, they are offered (voluntary) psychiatric treatment. This model is defended in the present book.

Incompetency Model (of coercive psychiatric care)   According to this model, only people who suffer from mental illness, who need medical treatment for it, who are not capable of making an autonomous decision about their medical needs and who do not assent to the treatment,

155

should be coercively treated for their illness. This model is defended in the present book.

Laissez-Faire Model (of treatment of drug abuse)   According to this model, unless people volunteer for care against their drug abuse, they should not be treated for it.

Life Rescue Model (of coercive psychiatric care)   According to this model, only people who suffer from mental illness, who need medical treatment for it, whose lives are put at risk if they are not treated and who do not assent to the treatment, should be coercively treated for their illness. This model is rejected in the present book.

Living will   This is an advance directive, legally binding, pertaining to the refusal of medical treatments at the end of life, euthanasia (if permitted), non-resuscitation and life-sustaining treatment.

Meddlesome coercion   This takes place when a patient is forced (or manipulated) into undergoing some medical treatment in a situation where the patient *can* make an autonomous decision in relation to the treatment, and rejects the treatment, or it takes place when a patient is forced (or manipulated) into undergoing some medical treatment in a situation where the patient cannot make an autonomous decision in relation to the treatment, rejects the treatment and is given the treatment, *not in his or her own best interest, but in the interest of the caregiver.*

Mixed Model (of forensic psychiatric care)   According to this model, people who commit crimes under the influence of mental illness are convicted in accordance with criminal law, but not sentenced to gaol; instead they are sentenced to psychiatric treatment. This model is rejected in the present book.

Modest coercion   This takes place when a patient is forced (or manipulated) into undergoing some medical treatment in a situation where the patient cannot make an autonomous decision in relation to the treatment, rejects the treatment, needs the treatment and is given the treatment in his or her own best interest.

Need Model (of coercive psychiatric care)   According to this model, people suffering from a mental illness, who need medical treatment for it and who do not assent to the treatment, should be coercively treated for their illness. This model is rejected in the present book.

Paternalism   To practise paternalism means to coerce, in his or her own interest, a person who has reached the age of maturity and who is capable of making an autonomous decision; paternalism is rejected in the present book.

Philosophical suicide   This is a rational suicide where the person who commits it has desires that are resistant to cognitive psychotherapy (he or she does not give them up when it becomes obvious why they are held) and beliefs formed in a reliable manner.

Rational suicide This act can be rationally explained in terms of the desires and beliefs of the person who commits it; a rational suicide reflects (in action) the desires and beliefs of the person who commits it.

Suicide We commit suicide when, actively or passively, we seek and bring about our own death, either (in extreme cases) for its own sake, or (more often) as a means to some goal.

Tragic suicide A suicide that is not philosophical.

Ulyssian coercion This takes place in accordance with a contract made by the person coerced, authorising the coercion in question, for a limited time, stipulated in the contract.

Well-behaved paternalism This is practised when a person is stopped from acting in a way that means that others will be harmed, *with their free and informed consent*; well-behaved paternalism is defended in the present book.

REFERENCES

Bayer, R., 'Public Health Policy and the AIDS Epidemic: An End to HIV Exceptionalism?', *New England Journal of Medicine*, Vol. 324, 1991, pp. 1500–1504.

Beauchamp, T.L. and Childress, J.F., *Principles of Biomedical Ethics*, 4th edn, Oxford and New York: Oxford University Press, 1994.

Beck, J.C., 'Forensic Psychiatry in the USA and the UK: A Clinician's View', *Criminal Behaviour and Mental Health*, Vol. 6, 1996, pp. 11–27.

Bergmark, A., 'Ett lik i lasten? Om Lars Lindströms nya syn på behandling', *Nordisk Alkoholtidskrift*, Vol. 11, 1994, pp. 116–118.

Binet-Sangle, C., *L'Art de mourir*, Paris: Albin Michel, 1919.

Brandt, R.B., *A Theory of the Good and the Right*, Oxford: Clarendon Press, 1979.

Burti, L. and Benson, P.R., 'Psychiatric Reform in Italy', *International Journal of Law and Psychiatry*, Vol. 19, 1996, pp. 373–390.

Byne, W., 'The Biological Evidence Challenged', *Scientific American*, Vol. 270, 1994, pp. 50–55.

Capron, A.M. and Radin, M.J., 'Choosing Family Law over Contract Law as a Paradigm for Surrogate Motherhood', *Law, Medicine, and Health Care*, Vol. 16, 1988, pp. 34–43.

Cassell, E.J., 'The Function of Medicine', *Hastings Center Report*, Vol. 6, 1976, pp. 16–19.

Durkheim, E., *Le Suicide*, Paris: Presses Universitaires de France, 1930.

Dworkin, G., 'The Concept of Autonomy', in Rudolf Haller (ed.) *Science and Ethics*, Amsterdam: Rodopi, 1981.

Glover, J., *Causing Death and Saving Lives*, Harmondsworth: Penguin, 1977.

—— *What Sort of People Should There Be?* Harmondsworth: Pelican, 1984.

—— *Fertility and the Family: The Glover Report on Reproductive Technologies to the European Commission*, London: Fourth Estate, 1989.

Hamer, D., Hu, S., Magnuson, V., Hu, N. and Pattatucci, A., 'A Linkage between DNA Markers on the X Chromosome and Male Sexual Orientation', *Science*, Vol. 261, 1993, pp. 221–227.

Harris, J., *Wonderwoman and Superman: The Ethics of Human Biotechnology*, Oxford: Oxford University Press, 1993.

Hoshino, K., 'Bioethics in the Light of Japanese Sentiments', in Kazumasa Hoshino (ed.), *Japanese and Western Bioethics*, Dordrecht: Kluwer Academic Publishers, 1996.

158

REFERENCES

Hume, D., 'Essay on Suicide', in R. Abelson (ed.), *Ethics and Metaethics*, New York: St Martin's Press, 1963, pp. 108–116.

Isacsson, G., Holmgren, P., Wasserman, D. and Bergman, U., 'Use of Anti-depressants among People Committing Suicide in Sweden', *British Medical Journal*, Vol. 308, 1994, pp. 506–509.

Jackson, D.L. and Youngner, S.J., 'Patient Autonomy and "Death with Dignity"', *The New England Journal of Medicine*, Vol. 301, 1979, pp. 404–408.

Jensen, K., 'Mental Health Legislation in Europe', *International Bulletin of Law and Mental Health*, Vol. 5, 1994.

Kant, I., *Lectures on Ethics*, trans. Louis Infield. New York: Harper & Row, 1963.
—— *Groundwork of the Metaphysics of Morals*, New York: Harper and Row, 1964.

Langton, J., 'Mothers-to-be who Drink Face Detention', *Daily Telegraph*, 31 May 1998.

Lazar, N.M., Greiner, G.G., Robertson, G. and Singer, P.A., ''Bioethics for Clinicians: 5. Substitute Decision-Making', *Canadian Medical Association Journal*, Vol. 155, 1996, pp. 1435–1437.

Leenen, H.J.J., Gevers, J.K.M. and Pinet, G., *The Rights of Patients in Europe*, Deventer: Kluwer, 1993.

MacKellar, C. (ed.), *Reproductive Medicine and Embryological Research: A European Handbook of Bioethical Legislation*, Edinburgh: European Bioethical Research, 1997.

McKeown, T., *The Origins of Human Disease*, Oxford: Basil Blackwell, 1988.

Macklin, R., 'Moral Issues in Human Genetics: Counselling or Control?', *Dialogue*, Vol. XVI, 1977.

Makin, K., 'Court Puts Mothers before Fetuses', *Globe and Mail* (Toronto), 1 November 1997, pp. 1, 14.

Mann, J.M. and Fluss, S.S., *Legislative Responses to AIDS*, Dordrecht: Martinus Nijhoff, 1989.

Mathieu, D., *Preventing Prenatal Harm: Should the State Intervene?* Dordrecht: Kluwer, 1991.

Menzies, R., *Survival of the Sanest: Order and Disorder in a Pre-trial Clinic*, Toronto: University of Toronto Press, 1989.

Mill, J.S., *On Liberty*, in Mary Warnock (ed.), *Utilitarianism* London: Collins/Fontana, 1973.

Miller, B.L., 'Autonomy and the Refusal of Lifesaving Treatment', *Hastings Center Report*, Vol. 11, 1981, pp. 22–28. Reprinted in Samuel Gorovitz *et al.* (eds), *Moral Problems in Medicine*, 2nd edn, Englewood Cliffs, NJ: Prentice-Hall, 1983, pp. 63–72.

Miller, W.R., 'The Effectiveness of Treatment for Substance Abuse', *Journal of Substance Abuse Treatment*, Vol. 9, 1992, pp. 93–102.

Monahan, J., *Predicting Violent Behavior: An Assessment of Clinical Techniques*, Beverley Hills, CA: Sage, 1981.

Moore, G.E., *Principia Ethica*, Vol. 8, Cambridge: Cambridge University Press, 1903.

Munthe, C., *Livets slut i livets början* (The End of Life in its Beginning), Stockholm: Thales, 1992.

—— The Moral Roots of Prenatal Diagnosis: Ethical Aspects of the Early Intro-
duction and Presentation of Prenatal Diagnosis in Sweden, Studies in Research
Ethics No. 7, Gothenburg: Centre for Research Ethics, 1996.
—— Pure Selection: The Ethics of Pre-implantation Genetic Diagnosis (forth-
coming).
Murphy, G.E., 'Suicide and the Right to Die', American Journal of Psychiatry,
Vol. 13, 1973, pp. 472–473.
Murphy, J.G. (ed.) Punishment and Rehabilitation, California: Belmont, 1973.
Nozick, R., Anarchy, State, and Utopia, Oxford: Blackwell, 1974.
Pattison, M., Sobell, M. and Sobell, L., Emerging Concepts of Alcohol Dependence,
New York: Springer, 1977.
Plomer, A., 'Judicially Enforced Caesareans and the Sanctity of Life', Anglo-
American Law Review, 1997, pp. 235–271.
Reilly, P.R., 'Eugenic Sterilization in the United States', in Aubrey Milunsky and
George J. Annas (eds), Genetics and the Law III, New York: Plenum Press, 1985,
pp. 227–241.
Rhoden, N.K., 'Cesareans and Samaritans', Law, Medicine and Health Care, Vol.
15, 1987, pp. 118–125.
Rössler, W., Salize, H.-J., and Riecher-Rössler, A., 'Changing Patterns of Mental
Health Care in Germany', International Journal of Law and Psychiatry, Vol. 19,
1996, pp. 391–411.
Schumpeter, J., Capitalism, Socialism, and Democracy, London: Unwin, 1943.
Seneca, Epistula Morales, Vol. II, trans. R.M. Gumere, Cambridge, MA: Harvard
University Press, 1920.
Stein, E., 'Choosing the Sexual Orientation of Children', Bioethics, Vol. 12, 1998,
pp. 1–24.
Steinbeck, J., Of Mice and Men, New York: Covici-Friede, 1937.
Steinbock, B., 'Preterm Labor and Prenatal Harm – Commentary', Hastings Center
Report, Vol. 19, 1989, pp. 32–33.
Sverne, T., 'Comments on the Legislation Concerning Impaired Capacity and
Decision-Making in the Health Care Field in England and Wales, the Nether-
lands, Spain, and Sweden', unpublished paper 1997.
Szasz, T., 'The Case Against Suicide Prevention', American Psychologist, Vol. 41,
1986, pp. 806–812.
Tännsjö, T., 'Against Personal Autonomy', International Journal of Applied Philo-
sophy, Vol. 4, 1989, pp. 45–56.
—— 'Who are the Beneficiaries?', Bioethics, Vol. 6, 1992, ss. 288–296.
—— 'Should We Change the Human Genome?', Theoretical Medicine, Vol. 14,
1993, ss. 231–247.
—— 'The Morality of Clinical Research: A Case Study', The Journal of Medicine
and Philosophy, Vol. 19, 1994, pp. 7–21.
—— 'Ought We to Sentence People to Psychiatric Treatment?', Bioethics, Vol. 11,
1997, pp. 298–308.
—— Hedonistic Utilitarianism, Edinburgh: Edinburgh University Press, 1998.
—— 'Compulsory Sterilisation in Sweden', Bioethics, Vol. 12, 1998, pp. 236–249.
—— 'Informal Coercion in the Somatic Treatment of Patients Suffering from
Senile Dementia or Mental Retardation', Nursing Ethics, Vol. 3, 1999.

Unger, P., *Living High and Letting Die: Our Illusion of Innocence*, New York and Oxford: Oxford University Press, 1996.

van den Haag, E., 'Guilt Overrides the Importance of Death Penalty Discrimination', in Carol Wekesser (ed.), *The Death Penalty: Opposing Viewpoints*, 2nd edn, San Diego: Greenhaven Press, 1991.

van der Maas, P.J., van Delden, J.J.M., Pijnenborg, L. and Looman, C.W.N., 'Euthanasia and other Medical Decisions Concerning the End of Life', *Lancet*, Vol. 338, 14 September 1991, pp. 669–674.

van der Maas, P.J., van der Wal, G., Haverkate, I., de Graaff, C.L.M., Kester, J.G.C., Onwuteaka-Philipsen, B.D., van der Heide, A., Bosma, J.M. and Willems, D.L., 'Euthanasia, Physician-Assisted Suicide, and Other Medical Practices Involving the End of Life in the Netherlands, 1990–1995', *New England Journal of Medicine*, Vol. 335, 28 November 1996, p. 1699.

Webster, C. and Menzies, R., 'The Clinical Prediction of Dangerousness', in D. Weisstub (ed.), *International Yearbook on Law and Mental Health*, Vol. 3, New York: Pergamon Press, 1987, pp. 158–208.

Wittgenstein, L., *Notebooks 1914–16*, with a translation by G.E.M. Anscombe, Oxford: Basil Blackwell, 1961.

Youngner, S.J., 'Please don't Make Psychiatrists the Gatekeepers for Physician-Assisted Suicide', unpublished paper presented at III World Bioethics Congress in San Francisco, 1996.

INDEX

Act on Compulsory Admission to
  Special Institutions for Abusers 129
akrasia 12, 132
Annas, G. 124
assisted procreation 56, 62, 70, 145
autonomy of an individual's decision
  see principle of respect

Benson, P.R. 91 n. 1
Bergmark, A. x, 130 n. 1, 135 n. 2
Binet-Sangle, C. 34 n. 4
brain death 48
Brandt, R.B. 36 n. 7
Burti, L. 91 n. 1
Byne, W. 66 n. 3

Caesarean section 125
Cassell, E.J. 25 n. 1
castration 6, 9, 115
Categorical Imperative 40
clarity 3, 4
consequentiality 4, 14, 70, 127
consistency 4
criterion of rightness 2

Declaration of Hawaii 92, 94, 106–7,
  114, 116, 140
Donaldson, Lord 47
Down's syndrome 65, 68, 72
Durkheim, E. 33
Dworkin, G. 19

euthanasia 32, 35, 38, 39, 41, 46, 67, 155

Fluss, S.S. 19

Gevers, J.K.M. 19
Glover, J. 18, 63

Goff, Lord 46
habeas corpus 3, 99
Hamer, D. 66 n. 3
Harris, J. 63
Heliogabalus 112
Hippocratic oath 39
Hoshino, K. 22
Hume, D. 40
Huntington's corea 58, 68

Illich, I. 19
Isacsson, G. 37 n. 8

Jackson, D.L. 26 n. 2
Jehovah's Witnesses 24, 28, 95
Jensen, K. 19
Jesus 33
judicial security 3–4

Kant, I. 18, 40, 110
Keith, Lord 46
Kjellin, L. x

Laing, R.D. 19
lebensunwertig Leben 67
Leenen, H.J.J. 19
Levander, S. x, 115 n. 3
libertarians 8, 60, 76
living will 46–9, 102, 133

MacKellar, C. 20
McKeown, T. 101
Macklin, R. 63
McNaghten, Daniel 109
McNaghten Rules 109
Mann, J.M. 19
Mathieu, D. 126
Mathlein, H. x

meddlesome coercion 42, 43, 51–4, 139

Mill, J.S. 5, 9, 15–17, 18, 75, 76

Miller, B.L. 14, 19, 24, 25–6

Miller, W.R. 135 n. 2

modest coercion 51–3, 54, 139

Moore, G.E. 110, 111

Munthe, C. x, 65 n. 2, 118 n. 1

Murphy, G.E. 36 n. 6

Nazi practice 64, 67–8, 69, 119

Nozick, R. 18

paternalism (well-behaved) 76, 78, 82

Pattison, M. 130 n. 1

Peel, Sir Robert 109

philosophical suicide 36, 41

Pinet, G. 19

Plomer, A. 125 n. 3

principle of respect for the autonomy of the individual in decisions about medical care and social services (stated) 5

proportionality 123

Psychiatric Patients Act 96

rational suicide 36

Reilly, P.R. 70 n. 6

Remmelink Report 38 n. 9

Rhoden, N.K. 125

Rössler, W. 89 n. 2

Sanctity of Life Doctrine 40

Sandman, L. x

Schneider, A.J. x

Schopenhauer, A. 36

Schumpeter, J. 73

Seneca 40

Silfverhielm, H. x

Singer, P. x

slippery slope 38, 137

Socrates 33

Stein, E. 66 n. 4

Steinbock, B. 124

Strindberg, A. 99

suicide (tragic) 35, 37, 39, 41

Sverne, T. x, 19, 46 n. 12, 89 n. 1

Szasz, T. 35

Tännsjö, T. 45 n. 11

Thorpe, Justice 47

transplantation 48

Ulyssian coercion 132–3, 135, 137, 139

Unger, P. 128 n. 4

van der Maas, P.J. 38 n. 9

Wittgenstein, L. 41

Youngner, S. 26 n. 2, 34